A SCHOLASTIC
KID'S
Encyclopedia

TRANSPORTATION

Automobiles to Zeppelins

TRANSPORTATION

Automobiles to Zeppelins

June English

Scholastic Inc.

New York   Toronto   London   Auckland   Sydney

Design and Art Direction: Todd Cooper, Paula Radding, Ned Campbell / BILL SMITH Studio
Illustration: Moffitt Cecil
Advisor: Paul Forsythe Johnston, PhD, Washington, D.C.

Consultants: David Tantrum and Rik van Hemmen,
  Martin, Ottaway and van Hemmen
Editorial Consultants: Sue Macy; Julie Winterbottom
Photo Research: Beaura Ringrose
Editorial Research: Vincent Duggan; Patricia E. Kligys

For their assistance in the preparation of this manuscript, grateful acknowledgment
to Mimi George, Peggy Intrator, Carolyn Jackson, Pam Nelson, Grace How, Pat Treanor, and Bernard Shea

LIBRARY OF CONGRESS CATALOGING-IN-PUBLICATION DATA

English, June
    Transportation: automobiles to zeppelins / June English.
        p. cm. — (Scholastic kid's encyclopedia)
    Includes index.
    ISBN 0-590-27550-X
    1. Transportation — Encyclopedia, Juvenile. 2. Transportation.
I. Title. II. Series.
TA1149.E55   1195
629.04 — dc20   94-29245
                                                                     CIP
                                                                     AC

12 11 10 9 8 7 6 5 4 3 2 1   5 6 7 8 9/0/09

Printed in the U.S.A.
First Scholastic printing, March 1995

Table of Contents

Introduction

THIS BOOK is all about transportation—the way we get around on land, on and under the water, in the air, and in space. Of course, the simplest means of transportation is walking, but it requires a human being to do all the work. Early in human history, people tamed animals to help them move and carry things from place to place. They built vehicles, such as sleds and simple wheeled carts that animals could pull. Eventually, people built engines to replace animals as a source of power. Though simple vehicles are still used in parts of the world, much faster and more powerful ways of travel have developed over the last hundred years.

Lots of things affect when vehicles get built and become a part of our lives. Leonardo da Vinci thought up the idea of a helicopter in the late 1400s, but his idea only got into the air in 1939. The helicopter he imagined needed lightweight materials and a small, powerful engine. Those things were not available until the twentieth century.

The time between when an idea springs up and when it becomes reality seems to be shrinking. In 1870, the writer Jules Verne in *Twenty Thousand Leagues Under the Sea* described a submarine called the *Nautilus* with a strange source of energy similar to nuclear power. The first actual nuclear submarine, called the *U.S.S. Nautilus*, was launched in 1954.

Engineers and inventors are constantly working on new means of transportation. Often, there is a very good reason why a vehicle is created at a certain time. Wars, for instance, often call for new designs from inventors. Many of the vehicles we travel in now were first designed for military use. Jets, tractors, and rockets were all developed during wars. Exploration, on Earth and in space, has also inspired many different vehicles—from the caravel ships of Columbus to the space shuttle.

Today, we dream about traveling into deep space in starships. Scientists are already developing ideas for fuels and engines that can power vehicles over such long distances.

Still, some of the greatest inventions have come from people just having fun. Orville and Wilbur Wright worked for years to get their *Flyer* into the air just for the simple thrill of flying. Almost no one believed a helicopter would be good for anything. But Igor Sikorsky worked on his design until he proved the doubters wrong.

HOW TRANSPORTATION CHANGES CHANGE OUR LIVES

The development of new kinds of vehicles almost always changes the way we live. Two hundred years ago, if you wanted to get from New York City to Paris, you would have to take a long voyage by ship across the Atlantic Ocean and then an overland trip by horse and carriage. It would probably have taken you several months. The journey across sea and land would have been dirty, difficult, expensive, and dangerous.

Today, on the other hand, you can travel from New York to Paris by jet in about the same number of hours as a school day. A supersonic jet can get you there by lunchtime— in just over three hours. Though the ticket still won't be cheap, your journey will have been a lot more pleasant and much safer.

Transportation not only changes how we live but where we live. Whole new towns grew up around the railroads that were built in the late 1800s. Superhighways, built after World War II, made possible the growth of suburbs around cities. Today, transportation experts are looking for solutions to the traffic jams our many automobiles create. By the time you grow up, they may be a thing of the past.

HOW TO USE THIS BOOK

All the vehicles included in this book are listed by type, so it's easy to find the vehicle you want to read about. Each vehicle has an icon (**A**) next to its title. The icon tells you whether the vehicle is used on the water, on land, in the air, or in space. Each vehicle also has a diagram that will show you its basic parts (**B**).

Say you want to learn everything you can about airplanes. Start at the AIRPLANES pages and keep on reading. You'll learn about all kinds of planes—from supersonic jets to tiny ultralights. Under AIRPLANES—WORKING, you'll read about how planes are used to do special jobs. You'll also see what aircraft in the future might be like under AIRPLANES—In the Future. If you

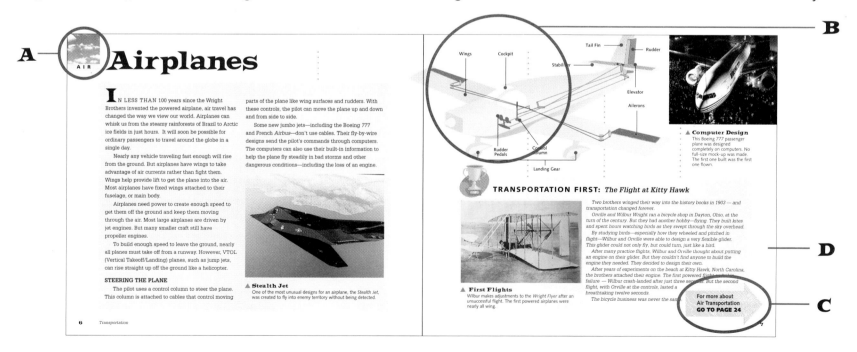

A

Airplanes

I N LESS THAN 100 years since the Wright Brothers invented the powered airplane, air travel has changed the way we view our world. Airplanes can whisk us from the steamy rainforests of Brazil to Arctic ice fields in just hours. It will soon be possible for ordinary passengers to travel around the globe in a single day.

Nearly any vehicle traveling fast enough will rise from the ground. But airplanes have wings to take advantage of air currents rather than fight them. Wings help provide lift to get the plane into the air. Most airplanes have fixed wings attached to their fuselage, or main body.

Airplanes need power to create enough speed to get them off the ground and keep them moving through the air. Most large airplanes are driven by jet engines. But many smaller craft still have propeller engines.

To build enough speed to leave the ground, nearly all planes must take off from a runway. However, VTOL (Vertical Takeoff/Landing) planes, such as jump jets, can rise straight up off the ground like a helicopter.

STEERING THE PLANE

The pilot uses a control column to steer the plane. This column is attached to cables that control moving parts of the plane like wing surfaces and rudders. With these controls, the pilot can move the plane up and down and from side to side.

Some new jumbo jets—including the Boeing 777 and French *Airbus*—don't use cables. Their fly-by-wire designs send the pilot's commands through computers. The computers can also use their built-in information to help the plane fly steadily in bad storms and other dangerous conditions—including the loss of an engine.

▲ **Stealth Jet**
One of the most unusual designs for an airplane, the *Stealth Jet*, was created to fly into enemy territory without being detected.

B

Tail Fin
Rudder
Wings
Cockpit
Stabilizer
Elevator
Ailerons
Rudder Pedals
Control Column
Landing Gear

▲ **Computer Design**
This Boeing 777 passenger plane was designed completely on computers. No full-size mock-up was made. The first one built was the first one flown.

TRANSPORTATION FIRST: *The Flight at Kitty Hawk*

▲ **First Flights**
Wilbur makes adjustments to the *Wright Flyer* after an unsuccessful flight. The first powered airplanes were nearly all wing.

Two brothers winged their way into the history books in 1903 — and transportation changed forever.

Orville and Wilbur Wright ran a bicycle shop in Dayton, Ohio, at the turn of the century. But they had another hobby—flying. They built kites and spent hours watching birds as they swept through the sky overhead.

By studying birds—especially how they wheeled and pitched in flight—Wilbur and Orville were able to design a very flexible glider. This glider could not only fly, but could turn, just like a bird.

After many practice flights, Wilbur and Orville thought about putting an engine on their glider. But they couldn't find anyone to build the engine they needed. They decided to design their own.

After years of experiments on the beach at Kitty Hawk, North Carolina, the brothers attached their engine. The first powered flight ended in failure — Wilbur crash-landed after just three seconds. But the second flight, with Orville at the controls, lasted a breathtaking twelve seconds.

The bicycle business was never the same.

D

For more about
Air Transportation
GO TO PAGE 24

C

6   Transportation

7

want to know even more about airplanes, you can follow the arrows (**C**) to more information about AIR TRAVEL. And you can also check out AIRPORTS.

In **Transportation Firsts**, (**D**) you can read about how different vehicles were invented and why some didn't work very well at first. In **A Look Into History**, you can find out about the role various vehicles have played in human history.

Suppose you want to know about a special kind of airplane—a glider. In the Table of Contents, you will find an entry for AIRPLANES—Gliders on Page 8. What if the type of vehicle you are looking for is not in the Table of Contents? Maglevs, for example. In that case, you can look under M in the alphabetical Index at the

Timeline

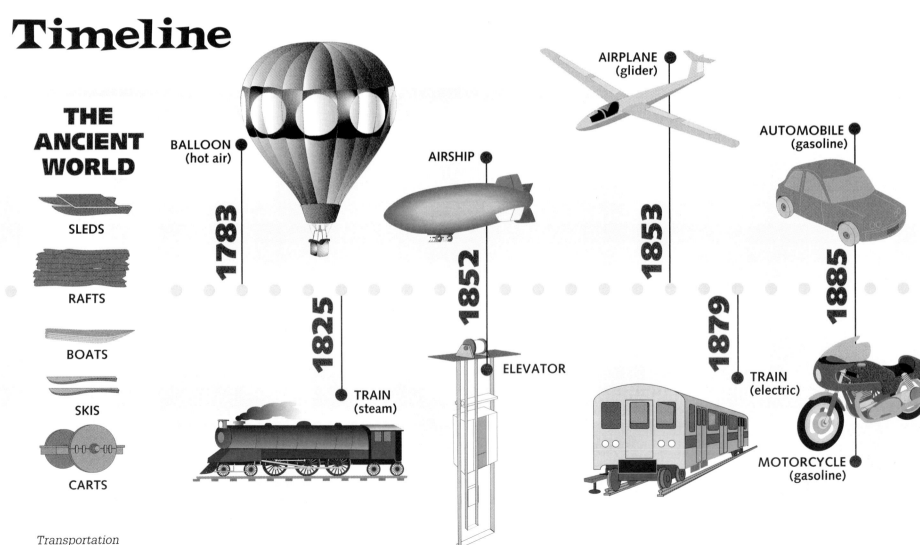

THE ANCIENT WORLD

SLEDS

RAFTS

BOATS

SKIS

CARTS

BALLOON (hot air)
1783

TRAIN (steam)
1825

AIRSHIP
1852

ELEVATOR

AIRPLANE (glider)
1853

TRAIN (electric)
1879

AUTOMOBILE (gasoline)
1885

MOTORCYCLE (gasoline)

back of the book. You'll see that one place to find Maglevs is on page 120 under Trains— High Speed.

This book also includes a Timeline on pages 4 and 5. Here you can see when vehicles were invented, and the order in which they came about.

Although this book works as a reference, it's also fun to read. You may discover some vehicles you didn't know about. You can see what some future vehicles such as the aircar or the spaceplane may look like and how they might be used. And who knows? Maybe one day you'll come up with some transportation ideas of your own!

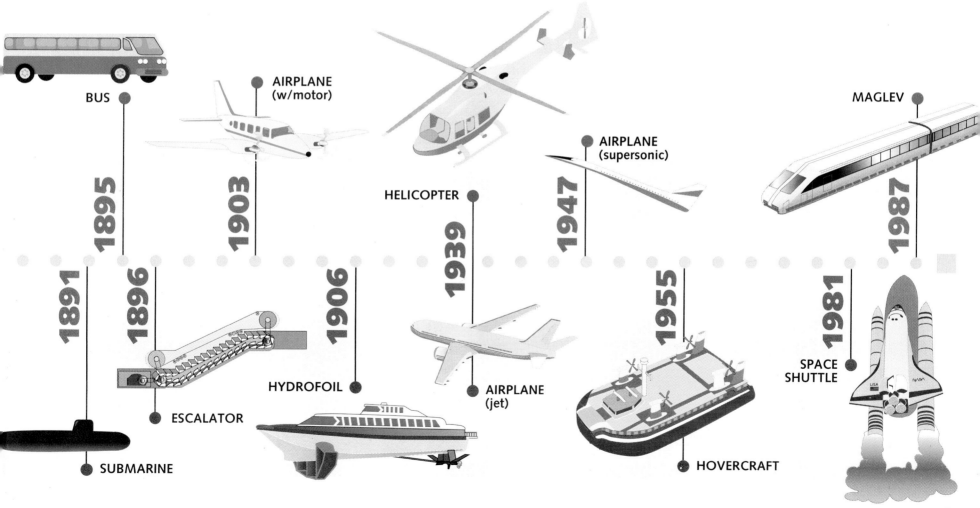

BUS

AIRPLANE (w/motor)

MAGLEV

HELICOPTER

AIRPLANE (supersonic)

1895

1903

1987

1891

1896

1939

1906

1947

1981

1955

HYDROFOIL

SUBMARINE

ESCALATOR

AIRPLANE (jet)

SPACE SHUTTLE

HOVERCRAFT

5

Airplanes

IN LESS THAN 100 years since the Wright Brothers invented the powered airplane, air travel has changed the way we view our world. Airplanes can whisk us from the steamy rainforests of Brazil to Arctic ice fields in just hours. It will soon be possible for ordinary passengers to travel around the globe in a single day.

Nearly any vehicle traveling fast enough will rise from the ground. But airplanes have wings to take advantage of air currents rather than fight them. Wings help provide lift to get the plane into the air. Most airplanes have fixed wings attached to their fuselage, or main body.

Airplanes need power to create enough speed to get them off the ground and keep them moving through the air. Most large airplanes are driven by jet engines. But many smaller craft still have propeller engines.

To build enough speed to leave the ground, nearly all planes must take off from a runway. However, VTOL (Vertical Takeoff/Landing) planes, such as jump jets, can rise straight up off the ground like a helicopter.

STEERING THE PLANE

The pilot uses a control column to steer the plane. This column is attached to cables that control moving parts of the plane like wing surfaces and rudders. With these controls, the pilot can move the plane up and down and from side to side.

Some new jumbo jets—including the Boeing *777* and French *Airbus*—don't use cables. Their fly-by-wire designs send the pilot's commands through computers. The computers can also use their built-in information to help the plane fly steadily in bad storms and other dangerous conditions—including the loss of an engine.

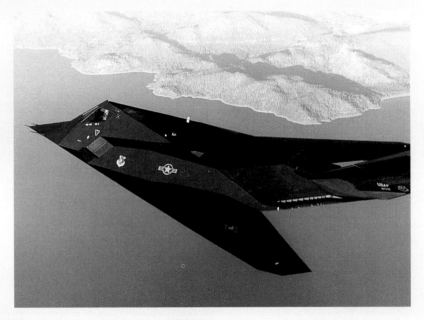

▲ Stealth Jet
One of the most unusual designs for an airplane, the *Stealth Jet*, was created to fly into enemy territory without being detected.

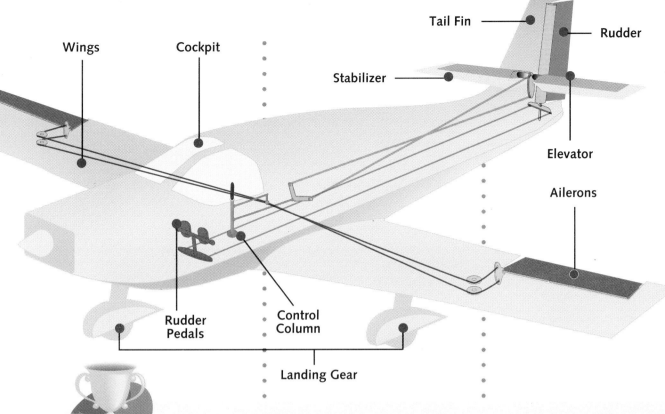

Wings

Cockpit

Tail Fin

Rudder

Stabilizer

Elevator

Ailerons

Rudder Pedals

Control Column

Landing Gear

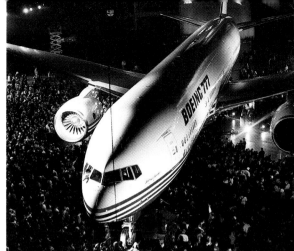

▲ Computer Design

This Boeing *777* passenger plane was designed completely on computers. No full-size mock-up was made. The first one built was the first one flown.

TRANSPORTATION FIRST: *The Flight at Kitty Hawk*

▲ First Flights

Wilbur makes adjustments to the *Wright Flyer* after an unsuccessful flight. The first powered airplanes were nearly all wing.

Two brothers winged their way into the history books in 1903 — and transportation changed forever.

Orville and Wilbur Wright ran a bicycle shop in Dayton, Ohio, at the turn of the century. But they had another hobby—flying. They built kites and spent hours watching birds as they swept through the sky overhead.

By studying birds—especially how they wheeled and pitched in flight—Wilbur and Orville were able to design a very flexible glider. This glider could not only fly, but could turn, just like a bird.

After many practice flights, Wilbur and Orville thought about putting an engine on their glider. But they couldn't find anyone to build the engine they needed. They decided to design their own.

After years of experiments on the beach at Kitty Hawk, North Carolina, the brothers attached their engine. The first powered flight ended in failure — Wilbur crash-landed after just three seconds. But the second flight, with Orville at the controls, lasted a breathtaking twelve seconds.

The bicycle business was never the same.

For more about Air Transportation **GO TO PAGE 24**

Airplanes ▶ Gliders

BEFORE the Wright Brothers learned to fly, they learned to glide. Gliders allow their pilots to experience flight as a bird does. In a glider there are no noisy propellers or jet engines, just the pure, silent thrill of sailing on the wind.

Instead of engines, gliders use air currents called thermals. These currents are created by hot air rising up from the ground. Birds use them to spiral high into the air. The glider's sleek bird shape helps it to ride these currents over long distances.

The fuselage of the glider is very narrow, and gets thinner toward the tail. This cuts down on drag, a force that reduces the plane's speed. Extra long wings add lift that helps the plane to rise. The glider's smooth surface is usually made from a very lightweight mix of glass and plastic.

Glider pilots can steer their planes just like powered aircraft. But since they have no engines, they need help taking off. Sometimes another plane tows the glider into the air. Or a car can pull the glider along until it's flying.

Glider technology is still a big part of airplane manufacturing. Even the high-tech Space Shuttle works as a glider when it lands.

▲ Gliders for Sport

Sport gliders, or sailplanes, often have very long wings, sometimes reaching 80 feet from wingtip to wingtip. When wind and weather are right, these planes can stay up for hours. In a dive, gliders can reach speeds of 150 miles per hour.

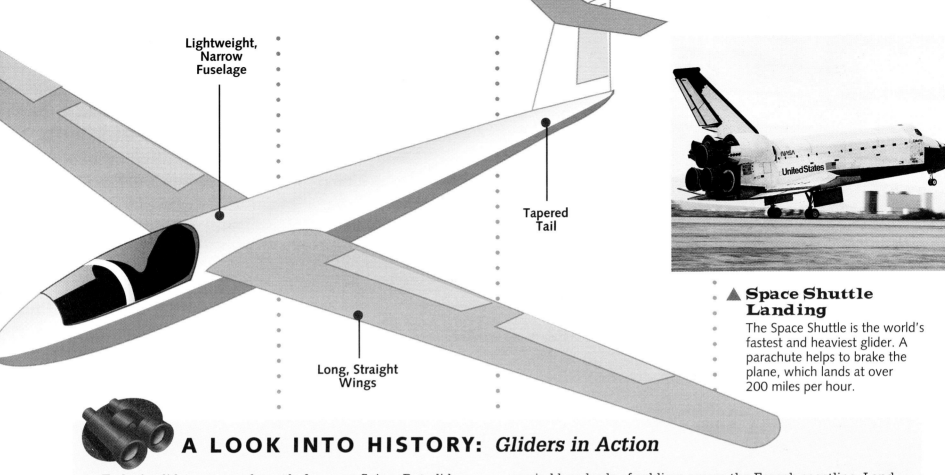

Lightweight, Narrow Fuselage

Tapered Tail

Long, Straight Wings

Space Shuttle Landing

The Space Shuttle is the world's fastest and heaviest glider. A parachute helps to brake the plane, which lands at over 200 miles per hour.

A LOOK INTO HISTORY: *Gliders in Action*

Today's gliders are used mostly for sport flying. But gliders have been used for other purposes, especially during wartime.

In 1944, during World War II, the Allied armies of the United States, Canada, and Great Britain were getting ready to invade France, which was occupied by the German army. Thousands of German troops stood guard all along the French coast.

Landing soldiers along this coast was clearly dangerous. Even if the landing were successful, the Allied armies might be cut off by troops further inside France. In order to keep that from happening, the Allies needed to position some soldiers behind the German defenses. This was a problem, since landing troops with regular airplanes was impossible. All airstrips were already in the hands of the German army.

The Allies decided on two solutions. Some troops would be dropped by parachute. Others would be sent in on gliders. Gliders were silent and could land behind the German defenses without being detected. On the night of June 5, 1944, gliders

carried hundreds of soldiers across the French coastline. Landing the gliders in the dark was difficult and many soldiers died. But those who survived joined other troops dropped by parachute.

World War II Gliders

After death-defying landings, glider troops had to seize bridges and airstrips held by the enemy.

The next morning, Allied boats landed troops on the coast of France. The German army was taken by surprise. There was fierce fighting for several days, but the Allied invasion was a success.

For more about Air Transportation
GO TO PAGE 24

Airplanes ▶ Jets

THE JET ENGINE was created in 1930. Today, most large airplanes have jet engines. So do some small passenger planes. Jet engines are more powerful than propeller engines, so jet planes can be larger than propeller planes and still fly faster. The use of jet aircraft has made air travel less expensive and available to more people than ever before.

Jet engines work by sucking in air and mixing it with fuel. The mixture is compressed, or squashed, and blasted out again at bullet speed. This blasting force pushes the aircraft forward. Most larger jets are powered by turbofan engines. These engines work like jet engines, but use a large fan to pull in air.

The high speed of a jet also creates some problems. Jet aircraft experience a lot of drag, the force of wind that slows the aircraft as it flies. In order to cut down on drag, jet aircraft usually have swept-back wings. The shape of these wings helps the aircraft to move through the air more easily.

◀ Jumbo Jets

The Boeing *747* jumbo jet can hold up to 566 passengers or 850,000 pounds of freight. Its maximum speed is just over 600 miles per hour. A fill-up at the gas tank can take more than 50,000 gallons of fuel.

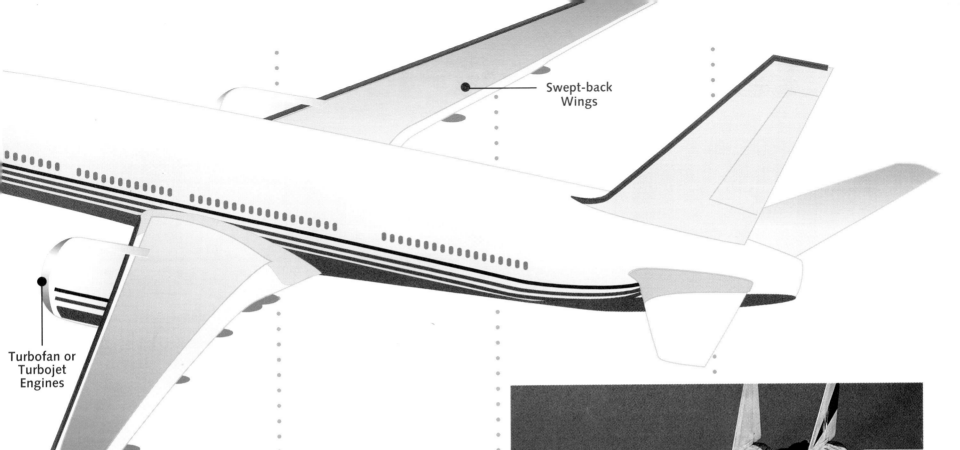

Swept-back Wings

Turbofan or Turbojet Engines

Passenger Plane Speeds

YEAR	PLANE	CRUISING SPEED
1910	Wright Biplane (propeller)	34 m.p.h.
1933	Boeing *247* (propeller)	189 m.p.h.
1940	Boeing *307* (propeller)	220 m.p.h.
1950	Douglas *DC6* (propeller)	280 m.p.h.
1955	Douglas *DC7* (propeller)	335 m.p.h.
1957	Boeing *707* (jet)	600 m.p.h.
1969	*Concorde* (supersonic jet)	1,350 m.p.h.

▲ Military Jets

Jet engines were first used in military planes by Germany in World War II. Almost all modern fighter and bomber aircraft are jets. This F-14 *Tomcat* is a classic fighter.

For more about
Air Transportation
GO TO PAGE 24

Airplanes ▸ Propellers

FROM THE first flight of the Wright Brothers in 1903 until the creation of the jet airplane in 1939, all planes were driven by propellers. Many of the first great flights—including the first transatlantic and transpacific crossings—were made by propeller planes.

At low speeds, propeller planes are more efficient than jets. And they can be maneuvered more easily. Propellers are used for light aircraft that fly short distances. And they're used for planes like fire fighters, crop dusters, and some cargo planes. They are easy to service and can land on shorter runways than jets.

Turboprop engines combine the best features of propeller engines with the speed of jets. They can work at high speeds. But they are also efficient when the aircraft slows down. Aircraft manufacturers are also designing jet engines with propeller fans— propfans— at the back. The propellers may reduce the amount of fuel planes need by up to 70 percent.

▲ **Propeller Service**
Propeller planes service hard-to-reach areas where there are few if any roads or rails.

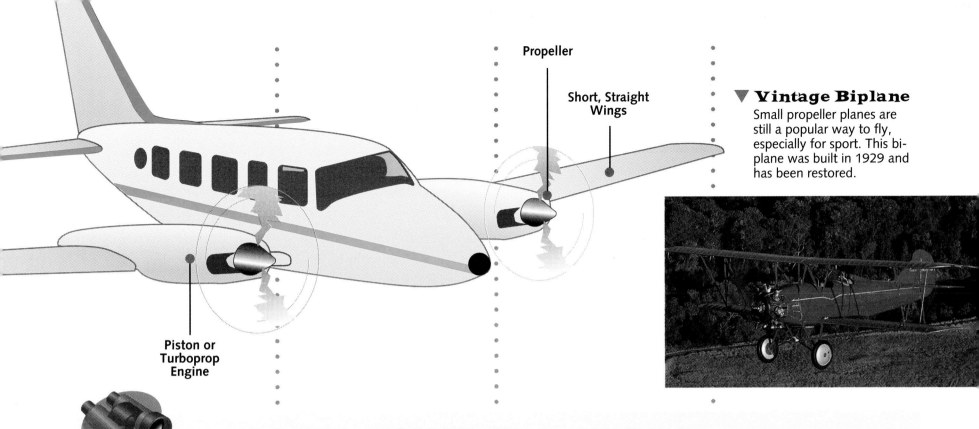

Propeller

Short, Straight Wings

Piston or Turboprop Engine

▼ Vintage Biplane

Small propeller planes are still a popular way to fly, especially for sport. This biplane was built in 1929 and has been restored.

A LOOK INTO HISTORY: The *Sopwith Camel*

In the Peanuts *comic strip, the character of Snoopy battles the German flying ace, the Red Baron. Snoopy's plane (really a doghouse) is called the* Sopwith Camel. *The Camel was a real fighter plane during World War I.*

As war raged between Britain and Germany in 1914, pilots from both countries took to the air. German flyers, in Fokker triplanes, had the advantage in these "dogfights." These well-designed German planes fired bullets through their propellers. (The firing was carefully timed not to hit the propeller blades.) With the planes, the German flyers, especially the Red Baron, downed most of the British fighters sent against them.

But in 1917, a new British fighter, the Sopwith Camel, *came into action. These propeller planes had not only their guns but the engine and fuel tanks all at the front. Although all this weight at the front made the Camels likely to fall into wild spins, they had some big advantages. They were fast and moved easily in the air. In just one year, the fierce Camels shot down nearly 1,300 enemy planes—though never the Red Baron's. He was shot down later by an Australian.*

▲ Propeller Fighter Planes

The real *Sopwith Camel* fighter and its famous imitator.

For more about Air Transportation **GO TO PAGE 24**

Airplanes ▶ Supersonics

Needle Nose

SUPERSONIC planes fly faster than the speed of sound. At sea level, that speed is about 1,088 feet per second, or 750 miles per hour. Planes that fly that fast create a shock wave called a sonic boom. It sounds like a thunderclap.

Vehicles that go into outer space and military fighter planes are supersonic. So is the *Concorde*, a passenger airliner that cruises at 1,350 miles per hour. Supersonic planes are not used for most flying because they use a lot of fuel, and, as yet, cannot carry large numbers of passengers.

Because supersonic planes move at such incredible speeds, they experience a lot of wind resistance, or drag. To reduce drag, supersonics usually have very sleek shapes. Many have special dart-shaped delta wings. The delta shape is very important in controlling the plane at supersonic speeds. As the plane reaches the speed of sound, the shock wave hitting the wing can make the aircraft hard to control. But the dart-shaped delta wing stays inside the shock wave so the pilot can fly the plane easily.

The National Aeronautics and Space Administration (NASA) is working on a space plane that may make use of supersonic speeds to travel around the globe in a few hours. The plane is designed to reach speeds of over 18,000 miles per hour as it enters orbit.

Supersonic speeds are listed in Mach numbers, named for Ernst Mach, a German physicist who studied sound. Mach 1 is equal to the speed of sound. Mach 2 is twice the speed of sound, and so on. Speeds between can be shown as decimal fractions. For instance, the *Concorde's* maximum speed is Mach 2.2.

▲ **The Supersonic Concorde**
The *Concorde* is the only supersonic passenger liner now in use. Because of its high speed, parts of the aircraft can get very hot. To cool off the plane's wings, jet fuel streams through them during flight.

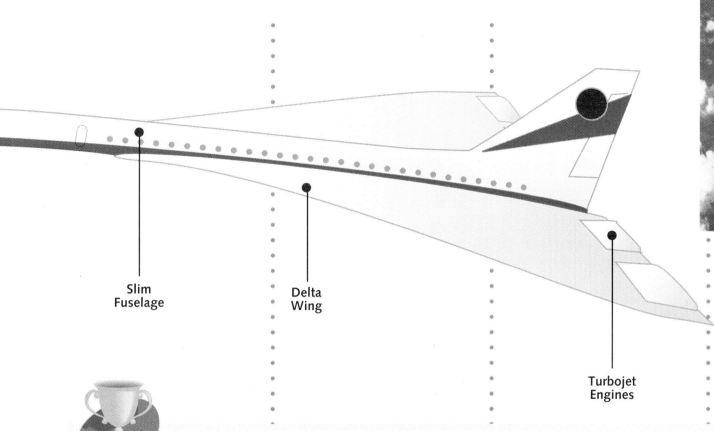

Slim
Fuselage

Delta
Wing

Turbojet
Engines

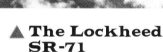

▲ **The Lockheed
SR-71**

The top-secret Lockheed *Blackbird* was used as a spy plane until 1990. It was able to cruise at Mach 3. The body of the plane was coated with a special black paint that was able to absorb radar waves. This made it very hard to track.

TRANSPORTATION FIRST: *Breaking the Sound Barrier*

As pilots who tested planes got closer to flying at the speed of sound, they got worried. Many people believed that a plane—or a person—would explode if they traveled that fast. Others thought that there was a real sound barrier. They believed this barrier was a kind of wall that would stop a plane trying to travel beyond the speed of sound.

Pilots couldn't help but notice that their planes would start to shake when they flew over a certain speed. Sometimes pieces of the plane would crack and break off. Pilots also noticed that their controls didn't work—or worked in reverse—at extreme speeds. A lot of flyers didn't want anything to do with "breaking the barrier."

But test pilot Chuck Yeager wasn't one of them. He believed that the speed of sound could be reached—and passed—safely. He took over the test flights for the Bell X-1 rocket plane. This was the airplane that had come closest to breaking the barrier.

By his eighth test flight, Yeager had come to within a tiny fraction of the speed of sound. He was convinced he could break the barrier with his next try.

The flight was scheduled for October 14, 1947. Two days before he was to go up, Yeager went horseback riding with his wife and fell off. He broke two ribs, but was afraid to tell the Air Force because it might cancel his flight.

On the morning of the 14th, Yeager could barely move. But he got in the plane with the help of a mechanic. He couldn't reach his arm across to the door, so he used a broom handle to close the latch. A few minutes later, Yeager, who had trouble staying on a 30-mile-an-hour horse, flew faster than the speed of sound—Mach 1.07. The supersonic age was born.

For more about
Air Transportation
GO TO PAGE 24

Airplanes ▸ Ultralights

GETTING into your own portable plane to go to school may seem like an impossible dream. But you could do it tomorrow if you had an ultralight plane.

Ultralights, or microlights, weigh much less than ordinary planes—usually about 200 pounds. They run on a gasoline engine so small it might power a lawnmower. Ultralights have wings similar to hang gliders that sit on a kind of tricycle called a trike.

These tiny, almost magical planes grew out of powered hang gliders. But the first models were so expensive, only a few people could afford them. An improved design lowered their price. Today people use ultralights for sport flying, but they also have a few practical uses. For example, archaeologists, scientists who study the past, have used the tiny planes to survey digging sites.

Advanced ultralights are a heavier version of the original ultralight. They may weigh up to 1,300 pounds. Many have small enclosed cockpits.

▲ **Ultralight Landings**
Since ultralights are so light, strong winds can buffet them, or blow them off course. Landing the tiny planes can be rough. Some ultralight flyers use a parachute to land.

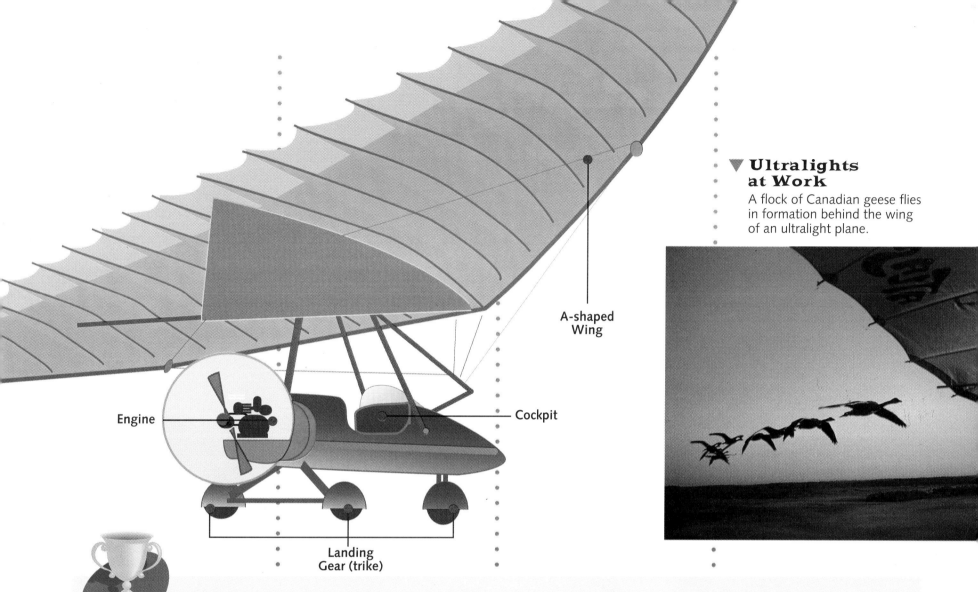

A-shaped
Wing

▼ **Ultralights at Work**
A flock of Canadian geese flies in formation behind the wing of an ultralight plane.

Engine

Cockpit

Landing
Gear (trike)

TRANSPORTATION FIRST: *Ultralights for the Environment*

People may have learned about flying planes from watching birds. But these days some birds may be learning how to fly by watching planes.

Bill Lishman, a sculptor from Canada, is a longtime supporter of wildlife. He's also an ultralight flyer. Lishman was worried that many bird species, such as wild geese, whooping cranes, and trumpeter swans, were losing their landing sites in North America. Birds were having trouble finding their usual migration routes. These are the paths birds take when they

fly south in the fall and back north in the spring.

Lishman thought he might be able to reteach some of these birds their migration routes. And maybe he could do it in an ultralight. Lishman started training a few birds to follow the sound of his ultralight engine.

Today he is successfully coaching flocks of birds to return to their lost migration routes.

For more about
Air Transportation
GO TO PAGE 24

Airplanes ▶ Working

BECAUSE THEY can move quickly from point to point, airplanes can do many jobs more easily and quickly than ground or water vehicles.

Seaplanes ●
have floats, or pontoons, that
let them perform rescues and
other work on water.

● **Aerial Fire Fighters**
fill belly tanks by sliding over
water. Then they fly to the fire
and drop the water on the flames.
Some helicopters are also used
to fight fires.

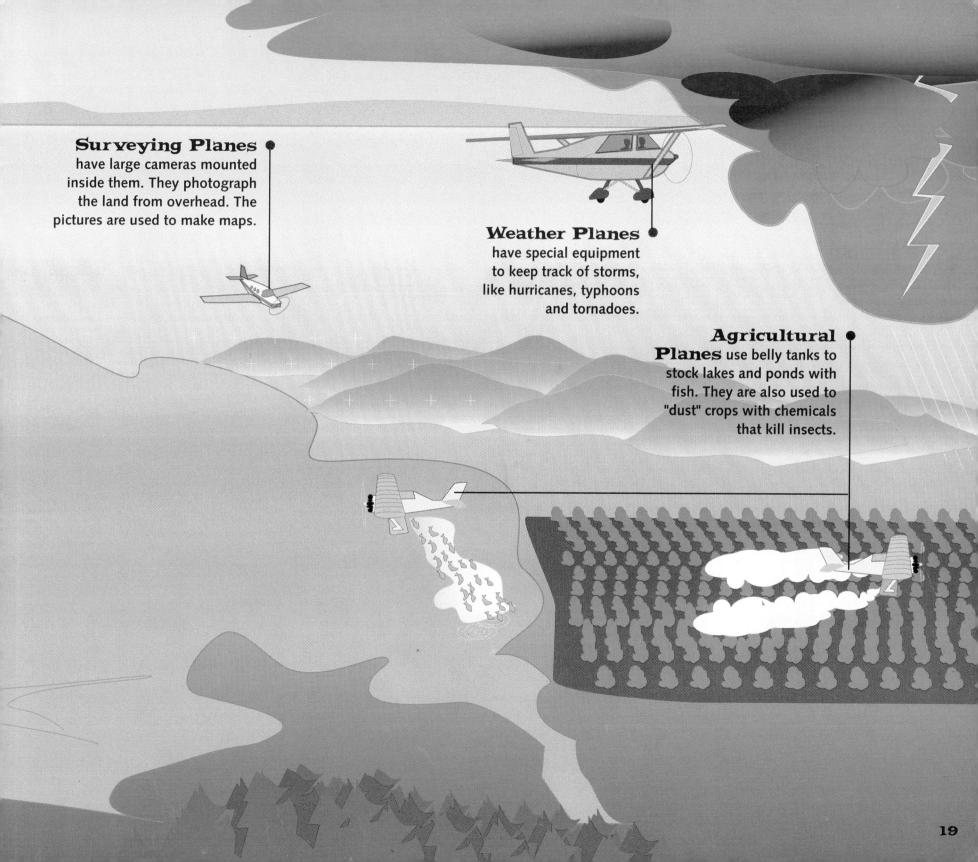

Surveying Planes have large cameras mounted inside them. They photograph the land from overhead. The pictures are used to make maps.

Weather Planes have special equipment to keep track of storms, like hurricanes, typhoons and tornadoes.

Agricultural Planes use belly tanks to stock lakes and ponds with fish. They are also used to "dust" crops with chemicals that kill insects.

Airports

AN AIRPORT can be a single building with one airstrip. Or it can be a large complex with many buildings and runways. An airport's business is launching and landing aircraft and caring for passengers and freight.

High in the **Control Tower**, air-traffic controllers keep track of the planes as they fly in and out. They use radar and computers to scan for aircraft all around the airport. Using radios, they give instructions to pilots. Other workers keep track of weather and ground conditions that might affect planes trying to land.

The main building in an airport is the **Terminal** at the end of the taxiways. An airport may have one or more terminals.

Inside the terminal, passengers can purchase **Tickets** and **Check In** for flights. Luggage is checked and run through a moving belt to be loaded onto the plane.

In a **Security Zone**, guards X-ray carry-on baggage and passengers pass through a metal detector to make sure items carried on the plane are safe. In large airports, passengers walk through a flexible tube called a **Jetway** to get from the terminal to the plane.

TICKETS

STOP

CHECK IN

TO PLANE

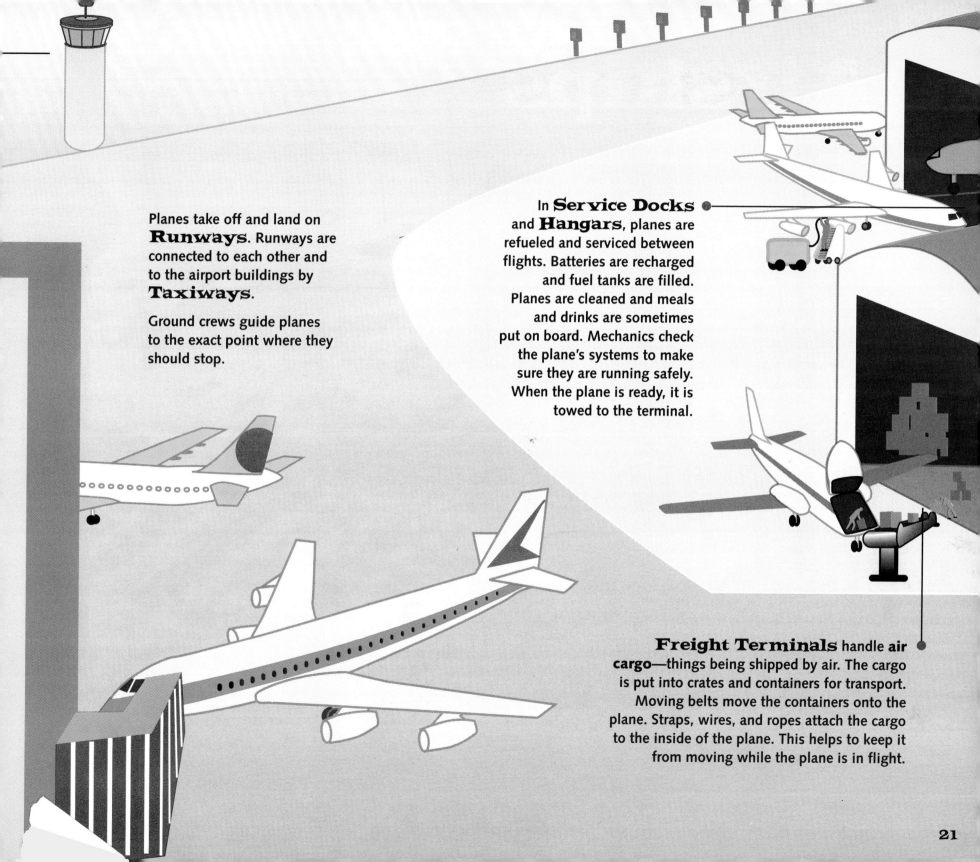

Planes take off and land on **Runways**. Runways are connected to each other and to the airport buildings by **Taxiways**.

Ground crews guide planes to the exact point where they should stop.

In **Service Docks** and **Hangars**, planes are refueled and serviced between flights. Batteries are recharged and fuel tanks are filled. Planes are cleaned and meals and drinks are sometimes put on board. Mechanics check the plane's systems to make sure they are running safely. When the plane is ready, it is towed to the terminal.

Freight Terminals handle **air cargo**—things being shipped by air. The cargo is put into crates and containers for transport. Moving belts move the containers onto the plane. Straps, wires, and ropes attach the cargo to the inside of the plane. This helps to keep it from moving while the plane is in flight.

Airships

AIRSHIPS work a little like party balloons that rise in the air. Both get their lift from a lighter-than-air gas, helium.

Airships are used for photography, filmmaking, advertising, and for scientific research. They patrol coastal waters and haul cargo. They are also being tested for rescue work. Airships can hover for long periods and, unlike helicopters, don't use lots of fuel when they stay in one place.

Inside the airship's envelope is helium, the gas that keeps the ship in the air. Under the envelope, passengers and crew ride in the cabin called a gondola. The pilot's instruments and control are housed here as well.

Some airships are rigid—they have a hard frame around the gas envelope. Other ships are flexible—they do not have a frame. They are sometimes known as blimps. The pressure of the air inside flexible airships helps keep the craft's egg shape intact. Most airships are made of synthetic fabric coated with rubber. They usually carry no more than 10 passengers.

Turboprop engines help airships take off and land and push them along in the sky. Unlike airplanes, airships can be stopped in midair by the pilot—or even reversed.

▲ **Airships for Emergencies**
The *Goodyear Blimp* gave emergency instructions to people after Hurricane Andrew in 1992.

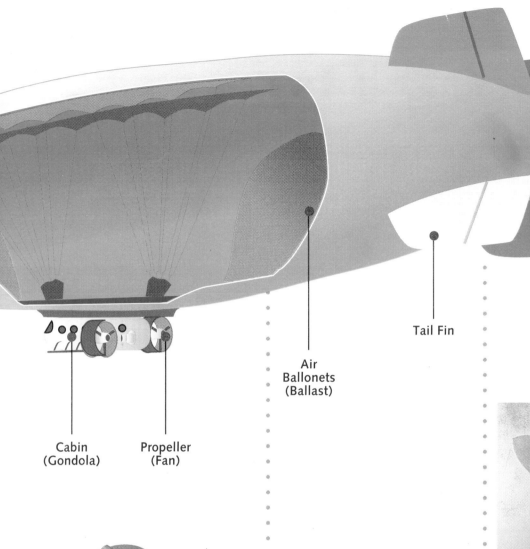

Cabin
(Gondola)

Propeller
(Fan)

Air
Ballonets
(Ballast)

Tail Fin

Rudder

▲ Airship at Work

Overhead shots of sports or other big events are often filmed by cameras perched in airships.

◀ The Hindenburg Crash

The 800-foot-long zeppelin *Hindenburg* crashed in May 1937, in Lakehurst, New Jersey. Though 35 lives were lost, more people actually survived the fiery crash.

A LOOK INTO HISTORY: *Airships for Travel*

The earliest flight in an airship was made by a Frenchman in 1852. Zeppelins, airships that were filled with hydrogen, were used by both Germany and Great Britain during World War I. Some were used to carry planes like the Sopwith Camel and other fighters. The first bomb to fall on civilians—not soldiers—was dropped by a German zeppelin in London in 1915.

Airship travel didn't really take off until the 1920s and 30s. During these years, German zeppelin "airbuses" carried passengers long distances in high style.

The hydrogen inside these airships made them dangerous, however, because hydrogen burns very easily. Several flights ended in disaster in the 1930s when the hydrogen gas caught fire. When the giant Hindenburg crashed and burned in New Jersey in 1937, the era of the giant airship ended.

Today the use of nonflammable helium gas in airships has made them much safer. One British company has begun to build airships for passenger travel.

For more about
Air Transportation
GO TO PAGE 24

Air Travel ▸ Basics

Taking Off

To fly through the air, aircraft must produce lift, a force that will move them off the ground. Aircraft do this in different ways. Some, like airships and hot air balloons, fill envelopes with hot air or helium gas.

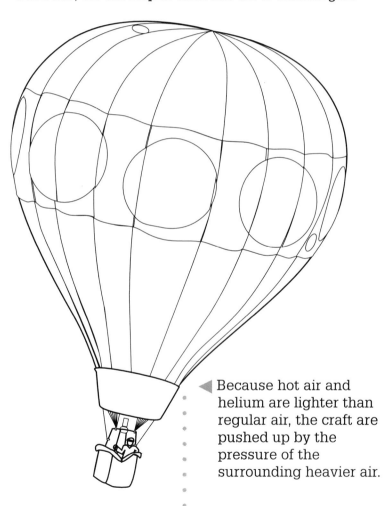

◀ Because hot air and helium are lighter than regular air, the craft are pushed up by the pressure of the surrounding heavier air.

Moving Through Air

IN THE AIR, planes are slowed by drag or wind resistance. Shaping the plane so that it slides more easily through the air helps to reduce drag.

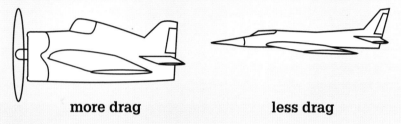

more drag   **less drag**

Wings are the basic shape of flight. As a wing moves through the atmosphere, the air around it lifts it. That's because a wing is an airfoil. An airfoil is a shape that can change the way air moves. It works like this:

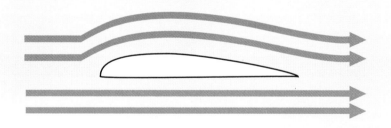

The airfoil or wing is curved. As air passes by, the flow over the top speeds up. But the flow underneath slows down. This creates pressure under the wing and makes it rise. The aircraft is lifted up.

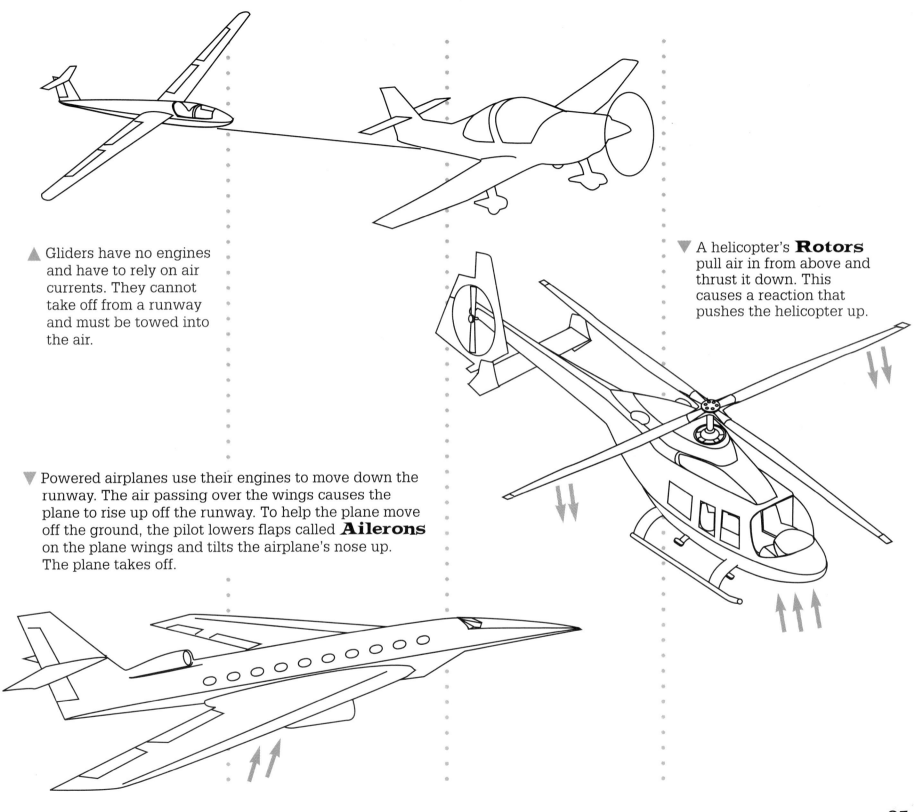

▲ Gliders have no engines and have to rely on air currents. They cannot take off from a runway and must be towed into the air.

▼ A helicopter's **Rotors** pull air in from above and thrust it down. This causes a reaction that pushes the helicopter up.

▼ Powered airplanes use their engines to move down the runway. The air passing over the wings causes the plane to rise up off the runway. To help the plane move off the ground, the pilot lowers flaps called **Ailerons** on the plane wings and tilts the airplane's nose up. The plane takes off.

Air Travel▸Basics

Controlling the Plane

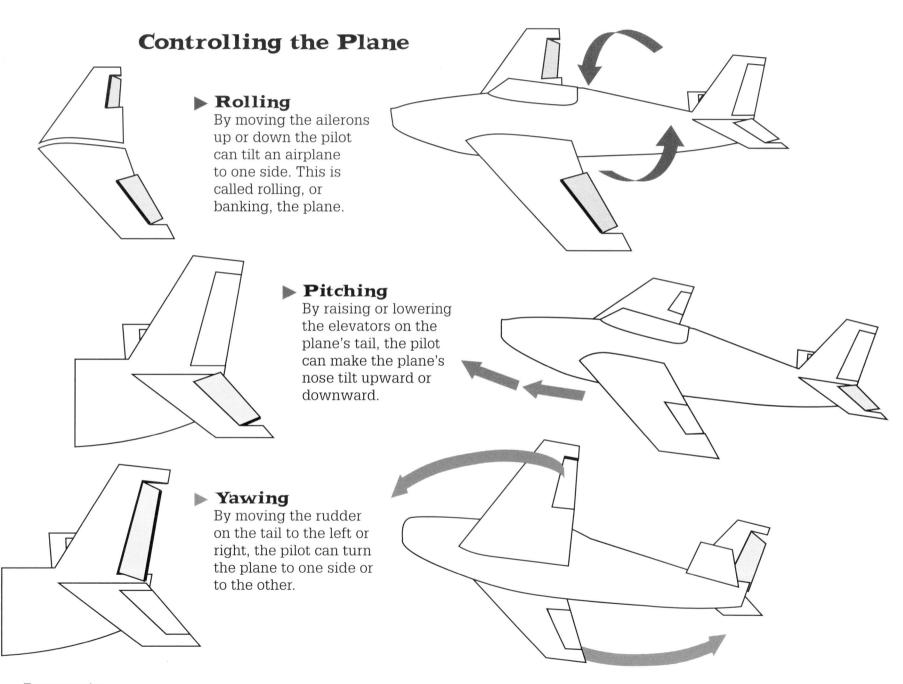

▶ **Rolling**
By moving the ailerons up or down the pilot can tilt an airplane to one side. This is called rolling, or banking, the plane.

▶ **Pitching**
By raising or lowering the elevators on the plane's tail, the pilot can make the plane's nose tilt upward or downward.

▶ **Yawing**
By moving the rudder on the tail to the left or right, the pilot can turn the plane to one side or to the other.

Landing the Plane

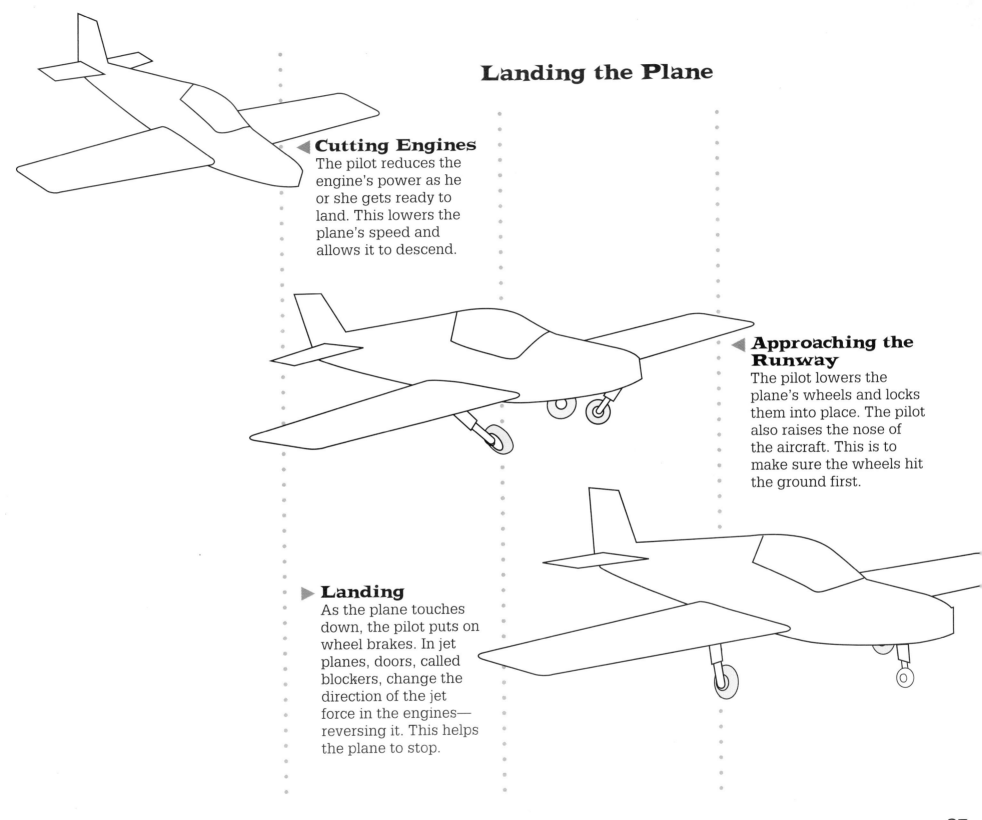

Cutting Engines

The pilot reduces the engine's power as he or she gets ready to land. This lowers the plane's speed and allows it to descend.

Approaching the Runway

The pilot lowers the plane's wheels and locks them into place. The pilot also raises the nose of the aircraft. This is to make sure the wheels hit the ground first.

Landing

As the plane touches down, the pilot puts on wheel brakes. In jet planes, doors, called blockers, change the direction of the jet force in the engines—reversing it. This helps the plane to stop.

Air Travel ▶ In the Future

AIRCRAFT DESIGNERS are always looking for ways to improve air travel. In the 21st century we should see some new kinds of aircraft. And we can expect new features on some familiar vehicles.

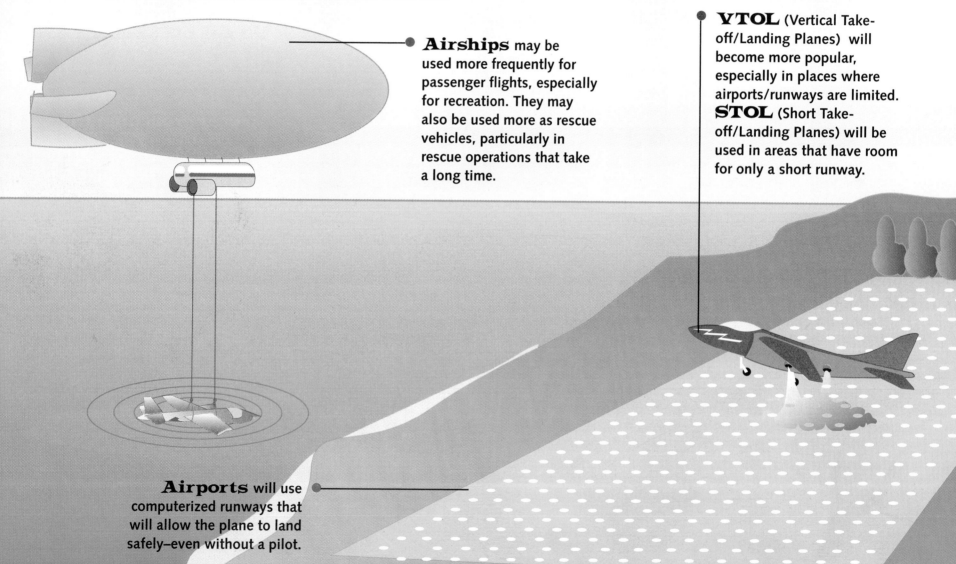

Airships may be used more frequently for passenger flights, especially for recreation. They may also be used more as rescue vehicles, particularly in rescue operations that take a long time.

VTOL (Vertical Take-off/Landing Planes) will become more popular, especially in places where airports/runways are limited.
STOL (Short Take-off/Landing Planes) will be used in areas that have room for only a short runway.

Airports will use computerized runways that will allow the plane to land safely—even without a pilot.

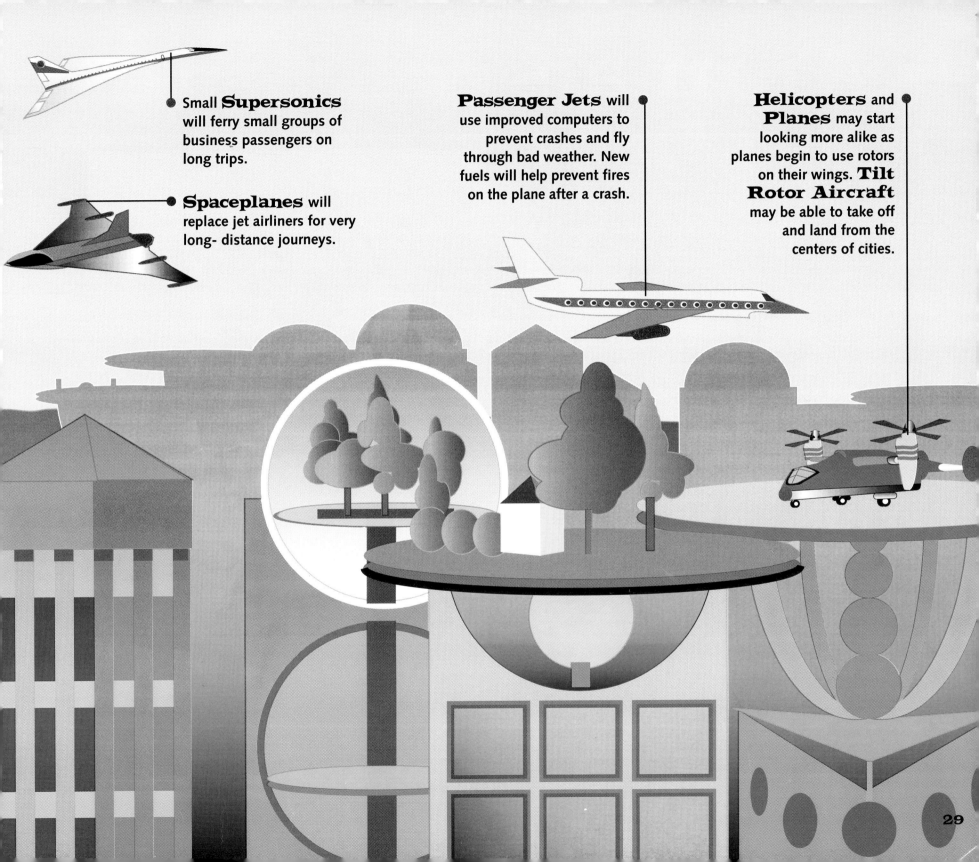

Small **Supersonics** will ferry small groups of business passengers on long trips.

Spaceplanes will replace jet airliners for very long- distance journeys.

Passenger Jets will use improved computers to prevent crashes and fly through bad weather. New fuels will help prevent fires on the plane after a crash.

Helicopters and **Planes** may start looking more alike as planes begin to use rotors on their wings. **Tilt Rotor Aircraft** may be able to take off and land from the centers of cities.

Animals

HORSES, donkeys, mules, camels, and sometimes elephants are used by millions of people for transportation. Animals make useful vehicles because they don't require expensive fuels, just food. And they can be parked easily.

Horses are used widely by ranchers, especially in North and South America, Australia, and Asia. They can reach speeds up to 40 miles per hour and work well with other animals.

Donkeys and mules are slower than horses but have other advantages. Though often quite stubborn, these animals can travel safely on steep slopes. They are used in mountainous areas in many countries.

Camels can travel longer distances without food or water than any other domestic, or tame, animal. And like some modern buses, camels can also kneel so that they can be boarded easily.

Animal Culture
The horse has been part of Mongolian life in Asia for over a thousand years. Kids sometimes begin learning to ride before they can walk.

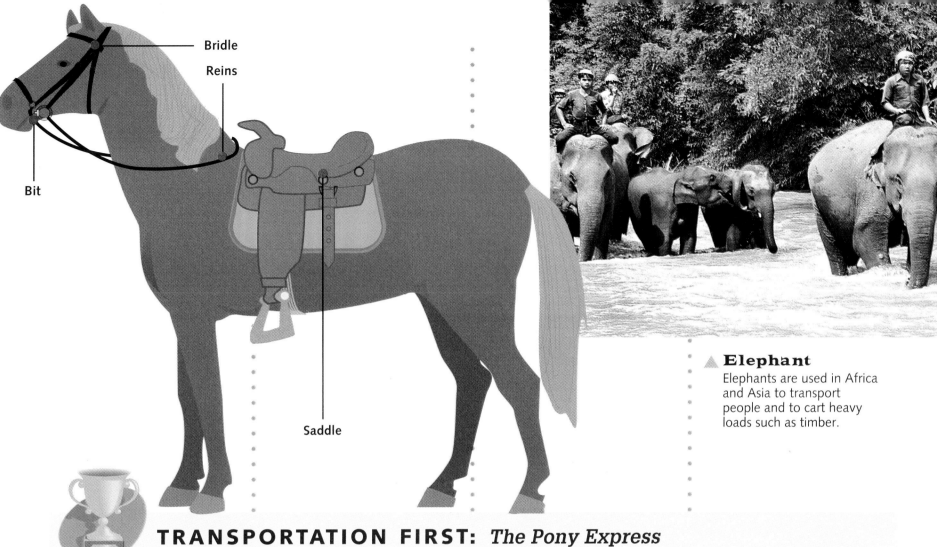

Bridle

Reins

Bit

Saddle

Elephant
Elephants are used in Africa and Asia to transport people and to cart heavy loads such as timber.

TRANSPORTATION FIRST: *The Pony Express*

Today express delivery companies make billions of dollars getting mail from here to there faster than ever. Overnight delivery across the country is common now. Some companies even offer same day delivery.

Many of the carriers providing express mail service around the world began in the United States. That would come as no surprise to the riders of the Pony Express. This service, which began in 1860, didn't provide overnight service. But it was an attempt to get mail to people in the speediest way possible. In 1860, that meant using horses and riders.

The Pony Express company built 157 stations on a route from Missouri to California. It bought 500 of the fastest horses.

Eighty young men, whose average age was 18, were hired to ride them. Each rider would gallop as fast as he could from his station to the next. There he would hand over his mail to the next rider.

This first express mail service was expensive. A 10-word telegram cost $3.50. A one-page letter cost a whopping $5.00—a lot of money in 1860.

The Express died out just 18 months after it started when coast-to-coast telegraph service began. Express mail service may just have been an idea 100 years ahead of its time.

For more about
Land Transportation
GO TO PAGE 86

Automobiles

WHEN automobiles first appeared at the end of the 1800s, most people believed they were a passing fad. But automobiles have shown no sign of disappearing. Each year over 47 million new cars are manufactured around the world.

Automobiles are usually fueled by gasoline engines. This engine transmits, or passes, power to the wheels of the car and they turn. The driver uses a steering wheel to direct the car's course.

Automobiles were invented shortly after the discovery of huge underground oil fields in the United States and other countries. This supply encouraged people to create many gas-engine vehicles.

Today, the underground oil supply is shrinking. And oil- and gas-fueled vehicles are a big source of air pollution. With more and more cars on the road, carmakers have had to make changes in them. For one thing, cars generally have gotten smaller and lighter. New, more efficient, and cleaner engines have replaced wasteful, polluting ones.

Until recently, most cars were constructed from steel sheets. But carmakers are using more high-tech composite materials to build automobiles. Composites are mixed layers of different materials like glass, carbon fibers, and resins. These materials can be molded into efficient, aerodynamic shapes.

Composite materials can be layered differently for special purposes. Some can be used to make tough car doors, or crushable parts like bumpers.

Fuels for cars have changed, too. Special chemicals are now mixed with gasoline to make it burn more efficiently, so it causes less pollution. Converters clean exhaust gases from some cars before they pass into the air.

Automobiles that use electricity and solar energy instead of gas are also being developed.

Solar Powered Vehicles
Alternative fuels like solar power will some day replace gasoline. The sunlight striking the solar panels is changed into electricity.

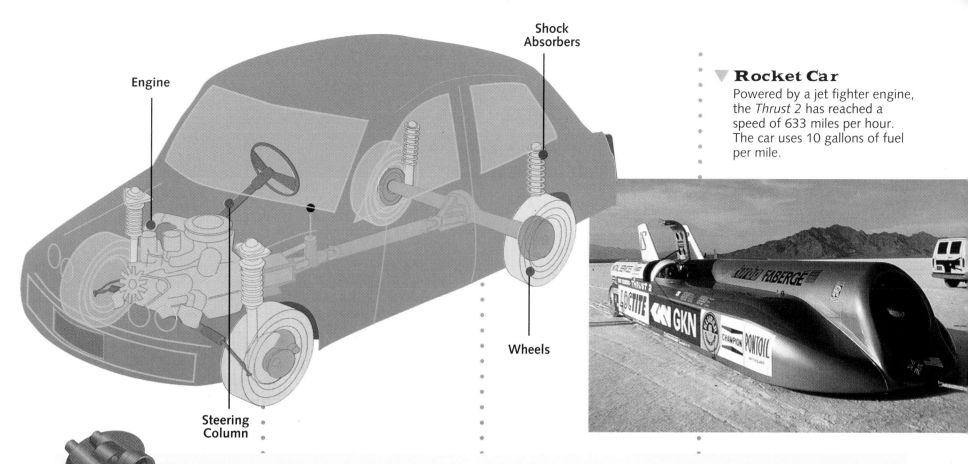

Engine

Shock Absorbers

Rocket Car
Powered by a jet fighter engine, the *Thrust 2* has reached a speed of 633 miles per hour. The car uses 10 gallons of fuel per mile.

Wheels

Steering Column

A LOOK INTO HISTORY: *A Car for the People*

At the beginning of the 1900s, automobiles were owned and driven by the rich. Henry Ford decided to change that. In 1908 he went into business building cars—and he wanted everybody to have one.

In order to cut the price of cars, Ford had to find a way to build them cheaply. He broke down the automobile into many simple parts that could easily fit together. And he began an assembly line where workers could fit the parts together quickly.

By building cars this way, Ford was able to reduce the price and pay his workers more than regular factory wages.

As expected, Ford motor cars were big sellers. Between 1908 and 1927, the company's Model T was purchased by 15.5 million people. Transportation—and the way people lived—changed forever.

The Model T
The first family car traveled about 35 miles per hour.

For more about
Land Transportation
GO TO PAGE 86

Automobiles► Designs

BECAUSE AUTOMOBILES serve lots of different purposes, they come in a wide variety of shapes and sizes. These are some of the designs you might see on the road.

Sports Cars are built for speed and handling. They have a sleek shape and ride close to the ground. Usually they have room for just two people.

Hatchbacks have a kind of lid or "hatch" on the rear that lifts up to hold lots of packages or even pets. These cars are good for small families. They're easy to drive and get good mileage.

Station Wagons have a storage section at the back for carting things such as groceries, bikes, strollers, or luggage. They have plenty of room for passengers and are good for large families.

Off-Road Vehicles or Sport/Utility Vehicles are rugged cars that can drive on the road—and off it. Their large wheels grip the ground and their high bodies make it easy to ride through mud or rocky fields.

Minivans are smooth-riding small vans designed to carry several passengers. They are also used by businesses to make deliveries.

Sedans are two- or four-door vehicles. They have powerful engines and wide seats that make the ride comfortable. Most use a lot of fuel, but new designs are more efficient.

Convertibles are great cars for pleasure driving. The top of the vehicle folds or rolls down. If the weather gets bad, the top can be put up again.

Automobiles ▸ Working

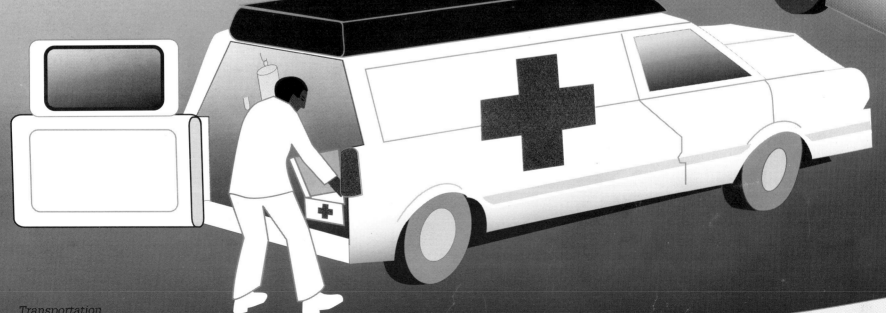

Ambulances
are designed like a van
with a large area at the
back where a stretcher
can be laid out and
attendants can care for
the injured person.

6645

PO

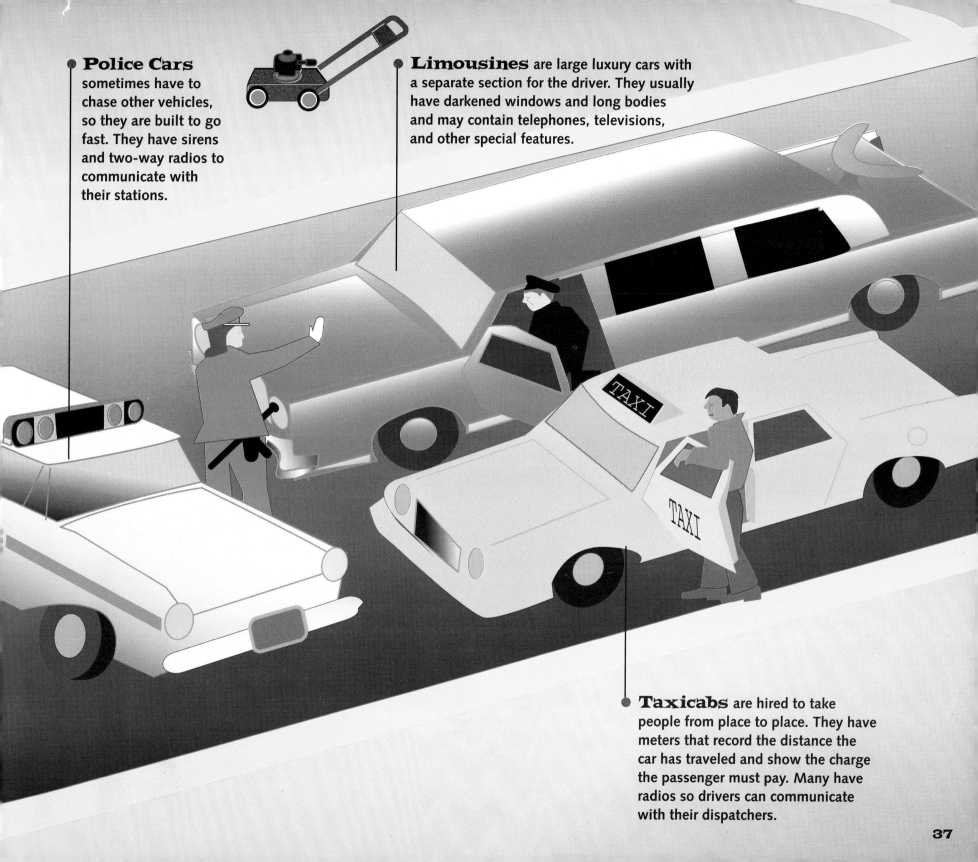

Police Cars sometimes have to chase other vehicles, so they are built to go fast. They have sirens and two-way radios to communicate with their stations.

Limousines are large luxury cars with a separate section for the driver. They usually have darkened windows and long bodies and may contain telephones, televisions, and other special features.

Taxicabs are hired to take people from place to place. They have meters that record the distance the car has traveled and show the charge the passenger must pay. Many have radios so drivers can communicate with their dispatchers.

Balloons

HOT AIR BALLOONS were the very first vehicles used for human flight. The first people to fly balloons were the Montgolfier brothers in France in 1783. (Even today in France air balloons are called *montgolfiéres.*) Balloons were used for recreation, photography, and other work for the next hundred years. During the American Civil War, for instance, Union soldiers perched in air balloons, searching for enemy camps.

When powered airplanes were invented in 1903, ballooning became less common. Unlike air balloons, airplanes could be navigated, or steered to land at a specific point. Air ballooning lost much of its appeal.

Improvements in balloon technology in the second half of the 20th century have made lighter-than-air vehicles like balloons popular again.

TWO KINDS OF CRAFT

Today two basic types of air balloons are used to carry passengers. The first kind gets its lift from heated air. Air heated by propane gas thins out and rises over the cooler, denser air, making the balloon rise. The second kind uses helium, a very lightweight gas, to get off the ground in much the same way.

Real steering in a balloon is impossible. But balloonists can sometimes control where their balloon will take them by riding air currents.

The Earth's atmosphere has layers like a big cake. At different heights, air currents may be moving in different directions. By changing the height of the balloon, pilots can often find a current going where they want to go.

The gas or hot air is contained in the balloon envelope. The part of the vehicle that carries passengers (usually a wicker basket) is called a gondola. Because balloons rely on light air for lift, all parts of the craft must be kept as lightweight as possible. To descend in the balloon, hot air or gas can be let out from a side vent or top port.

▲ **Balloon Rise**
Balloonists often take off at dawn. The cool, early morning air and lighter wind help the balloon rise more easily.

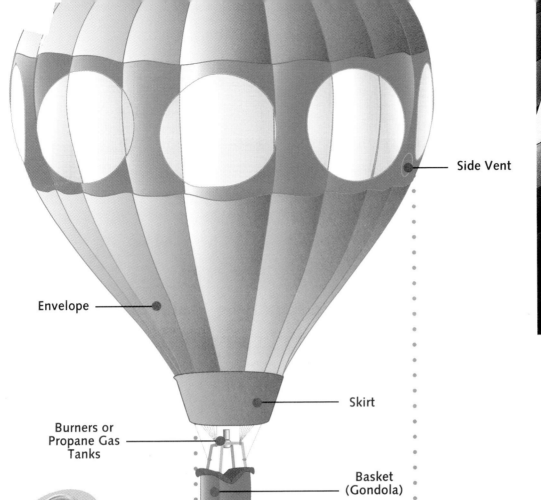

Side Vent

Envelope

Skirt

Burners or
Propane Gas
Tanks

Basket
(Gondola)

▲ Driving a Balloon

Each year hundreds of balloonists compete in the Albuquerque Balloon Festival in New Mexico.

SCIENCE CLOSE-UP: *Ballooning in the Jet Stream*

Both helium and hot-air balloonists have crossed the Atlantic and Pacific oceans. A voyage around the world is still to come, but balloon crews from several different countries are already making plans for it.

One way to get around the world quickly is to fly in the jet stream. The jet stream is a part of the high atmosphere where the air moves very fast. But air up in the jet stream is thinner than air closer to Earth. There isn't enough oxygen for balloonists to breathe, so they need a pressurized cabin just like airplanes have. The *Virgin Atlantic* Flyer used a pressurized cabin when it made the first hot-air transatlantic crossing in 1987. So did the follow-up Flyer that crossed the Pacific in 1991.

In the jet stream, air may move at up to 200 miles per hour.

Flying at such speeds is risky in a fragile balloon. Crews planning round-the-world voyages will have to have tough balloon materials. Some may use the same ultra-strong fabrics that go into bullet- proof vests.

No matter how strong the balloon is, the trip around the world will be dangerous. Most crews will probably take along some parachutes. Some may even use a kind of spacesuit in case the balloon breaks up high in the atmosphere.

Still, the trip would be worth the risk. Not only would the crew establish a record, but balloonists could take readings that would help scientists study storms and the ozone layer.

For more about
Air Transportation
GO TO PAGE 24

Bicycles

THE FIRST BICYCLISTS pushed their bikes along using their feet. Modern bicycles use pedals attached to a chain to move the bike's wheels.

Today, bicycles come in many different designs depending upon where they will be used—on city streets or dirt paths, for example. Frames are cut in different sizes to fit the rider. Most bicycles are built of steel. But bicycle frames may include any number of strong lightweight materials including aluminum, titanium, and plastics.

Many bicycles have different gears to let the rider move faster on level surfaces or climb slopes more easily. On multispeed bikes, derailleurs move the bike's chain from one gear to another. Some bikes have click-shifting gears. This means the shift lever actually clicks into position, letting the rider know the bike is in the right gear.

Bike brakes come in two varieties: caliper and coaster. Coasters brake the bike as you pedal backwards. Caliper brakes use two pads, or "shoes," to grip the rim of the tire and slow its motion. They are hand-controlled.

Bicycling is one of the cheapest and healthiest ways of getting around. It's good exercise, too, burning up to 300-400 calories an hour. That compares to about 60 for watching television.

Bicycling also helps protect the environment. Everyone who rides a bike instead of an automobile not only saves oil and gas but helps reduce air pollution.

All cyclists need to wear protective clothing—especially a helmet—in case of a hard spill.

▲ Country of Cyclers
Maybe more than any other people, the Chinese make good use of bicycles. They use them to go to work and school and for recreation.

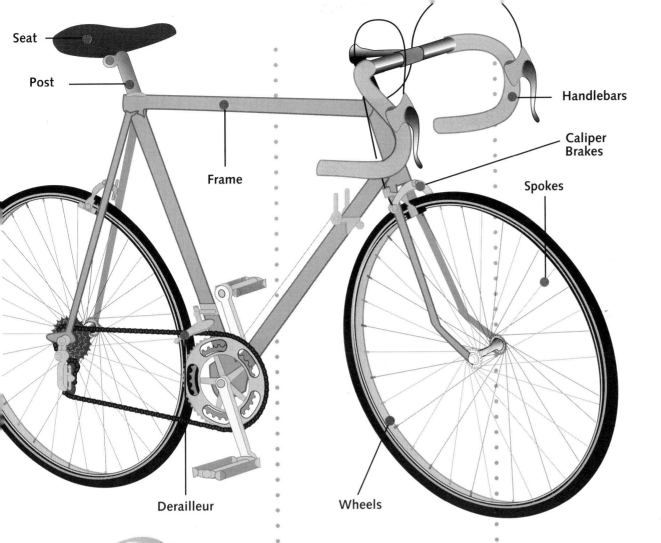

Seat

Post

Frame

Handlebars

Caliper
Brakes

Spokes

Derailleur

Wheels

▲ Bikes at Work

Bicycles are the perfect vehicle
for quick deliveries. They move
easily through traffic and can
be parked on the sidewalk.

SCIENCE CLOSE-UP:
How Bicycle Gears Work

*All bicycles have a chain that connects the pedals to the
rear wheel. This chain transfers the motion of the pedals to
the small rear wheel sprocket. Because the wheel is smaller,
it turns faster than your feet are pedaling. This allows you to
go faster even though the rate you pedal at is the same.*

*When you want to go uphill, though, you need a larger rear
wheel sprocket. That's so the back wheel can move with less
speed and more force. When you change gears, the bike chain
moves from one sprocket to the next.*

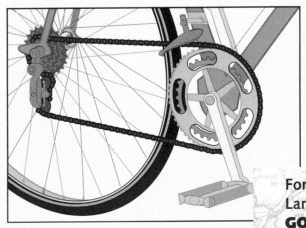

For more about
Land Transportation
GO TO PAGE 86

Bicycles ▶ Designs

BICYCLES travel nearly everywhere. But different types of bikes are used on different land surfaces.

Mountain Bikes have a sturdy frame and straight or "flat" handlebars. Fat, knobby tires give them good traction on trails and over gravel and dirt.

BMX or **Dirt Bikes** are made for rough riding and sport. They may have pegs for doing tricks like spins. They are built small and are usually used by young people.

Road Bikes are lightweight with "drop" handlebars and thin tires. They are fast and travel easily on pavement. But they don't ride well on rough roads.

City Bikes are a cross between mountain and road bicycles. They have lightweight frames, flat handlebars, and tires that are a little knobby. They can be used on pavement or dirt roads.

43

Boats/Ships

BOATS and ships are basically the same vehicle. But the word *ship* is often used for a very large boat.

The hollow shape of a boat and the materials it's made with allow it to float. That is because the surrounding water pushes up on the boat harder than the weight of the boat pushes down.

The main body of the boat is called the hull. The front end of the boat is called the bow. The back end is known as the stern. Most boats have a rudder, a kind of fin at the back that is used for steering.

Boats are powered in different ways. Some have sails attached to use the power of the wind. The simplest boats are rowed by people with oars. Today most boats and ships use some sort of engine for power. These engines usually use diesel or gasoline for fuel. A few now use electricity. Very large ships, such as aircraft carriers, may use steam turbines powered by nuclear fuel.

▲ Hong Kong Waterways
An endless stream of boats clutters the waterways in Hong Kong's busy floating market.

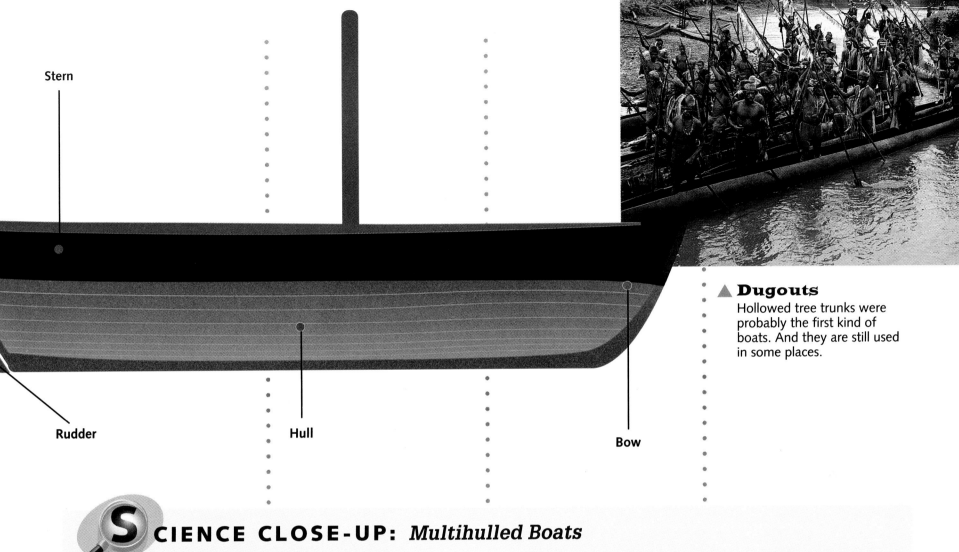

Stern

Rudder

Hull

Bow

▲ Dugouts

Hollowed tree trunks were probably the first kind of boats. And they are still used in some places.

SCIENCE CLOSE-UP: *Multihulled Boats*

Many boats have one hull, but multihulled boats are becoming more and more popular.

They were first built by island peoples in the Pacific. More than one hull gives boats added stability, keeping the craft from tilting over in bad weather.

Extra hulls also allow boats to move through the water more easily, increasing speed. Several records have been set by multihulled boats. One recent French boat design features four hulls!

◄ Hoverspeed Great Britain

This British *catamaran* (double-hulled boat) set a record for a transatlantic crossing.

For more about
Water Transportation
GO TO PAGE 132

Boats/Ships ▸ Aircraft Carriers

AIRCRAFT carriers are huge floating air bases used by modern navies. Large ones may carry over 6,000 crew and nearly 100 aircraft. The aircraft may include helicopters, fighter jets, bombers, radar planes, and submarine hunters.

The planes are stored below deck. Deck crews bring the aircraft up on giant elevators when they are needed. Blast shields help protect planes and deck crew from hot jet exhaust.

A carrier deck isn't long enough to be used like a regular runway. So planes are launched by a catapult, a track that works like a slingshot. And to land, pilots must catch a deck wire with a hook (fixed to the plane's tail). Flyers sometimes call this kind of landing a "controlled crash." That's because the plane comes in at over 100 miles per hour and jerks to a stop.

Planes can take off from the deck as often as once a minute, so deck traffic has to be carefully watched by officers in the control tower.

Aircraft carriers are usually powered by huge steam turbine engines. Some modern carriers now use nuclear fuel to power their engines. These giant nuclear carriers have most of the shops and services of a small town. They can travel close to 100,000 miles without refueling.

◀ **Deck Launch**
A catapult slings a fighter jet into the air at about 200 miles per hour.

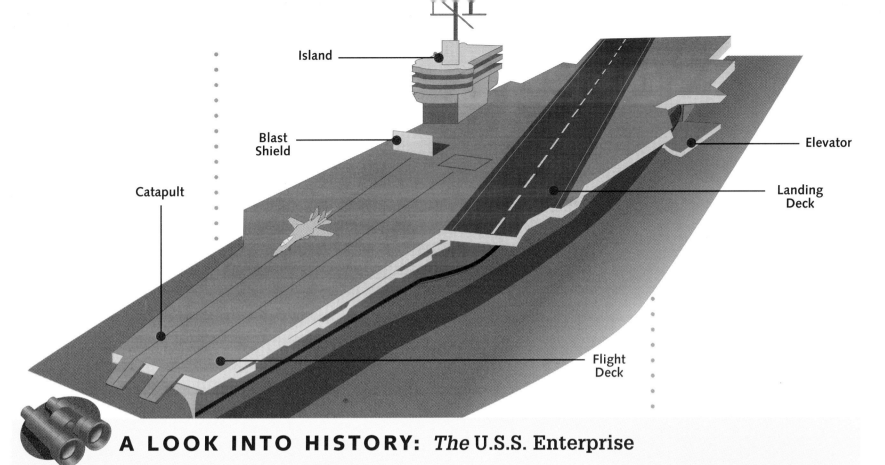

Island

Blast Shield

Catapult

Elevator

Landing Deck

Flight Deck

A LOOK INTO HISTORY: *The* U.S.S. Enterprise

Mention the name Enterprise and people might think of the Star Trek movies or television series. But long before Star Trek existed, another ship named Enterprise was staking its claim to fame—not in deep space, but in the Pacific Ocean.

In 1936, the aircraft carrier Enterprise set sail. Three years later, as the carrier's pilots were being trained, many nations around the world were at war. The United States was still neutral—but not for

U.S.S. Enterprise

The *Enterprise* crew surveys the damage after a kamikaze pilot crash. The giant hole in the deck used to be the forward elevator.

long. On the morning of December 7, 1941, the Enterprise was on her way back to Pearl Harbor in Hawaii. As she was nearing the islands, Japanese bombers staged a surprise attack, sinking or damaging many U.S. ships.

Though much of the American fleet was destroyed that day, the Enterprise was spared. It was a stroke of luck for the U.S. Over the next three years, the Enterprise and its aircraft proved vital to the U.S. war effort, shooting down over 900 enemy planes and destroying many Japanese ships.

Because of her success, the Enterprise became a main target for the Japanese military. Japan's forces successfully torpedoed the ship and hit it with shells. Kamikaze pilots (who crashed their planes and died in them) smacked into her decks more than once. But though Japanese radio reported her sunk seven times, she did, in fact, survive to become the most honored U.S. ship in World War II.

For more about Water Transportation **GO TO PAGE 132**

Boats/Ships▶Power

POWERBOATS include everything from a simple motorboat to a huge luxury liner. Instead of sails or oars, these boats use engines for power. The powerboat's strong point is that it does not rely on chance winds or rowers who might tire. Powerboats can be built larger and can go longer distances at greater speed.

Most small boats use gasoline engines for power. Outboard engines or motors are attached to the outside of a boat. Inboard engines sit inside the boat hull. Both types of engines supply power to a propeller. The force of the propeller cutting through the water and pushing it backward moves the boat forward.

Many small powerboats do not have a separate rudder to steer them. The fin on the back of the motor on the outside of the boat works as the rudder. Large diesel engines are needed to power big ships. Very large ships like aircraft carriers may be powered by nuclear fuel.

◄ Ocean Liners

Regular steamship service across the Atlantic began in 1840. Between then and 1920 more than 39 million people made the crossing from Europe. Today most people traveling across the ocean go by plane. But a few ocean liners still survive. The *Queen Elizabeth II* provides lavish service for nearly 2,000 passengers.

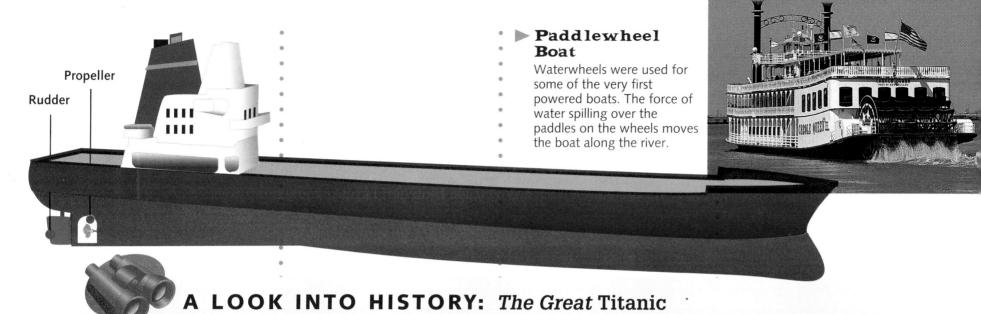

Propeller

Rudder

▶ **Paddlewheel Boat**

Waterwheels were used for some of the very first powered boats. The force of water spilling over the paddles on the wheels moves the boat along the river.

A LOOK INTO HISTORY: *The Great* Titanic

Just after midnight on April 15, 1912, the steamship Carpathia received a distress signal from another ship crossing the North Atlantic. The ship, the brand-new luxury liner, Titanic, had hit an iceberg and was taking on water. Though the Carpathia was some distance from the Titanic, the Carpathia's captain, Arthur Rostron, changed his ship's course, sailing as fast as he could to the Titanic's rescue.

When the Carpathia reached the Titanic's location at around 4:00 A.M., nothing was visible except the dark calm sea and a sky full of stars. Finally, the crew spotted a green flare shot up from a lifeboat. When the rescued passengers were hauled on board, Captain Rostron asked what had happened to the huge ocean liner. Perhaps he already knew the terrible truth. The Titanic had sunk. With her had gone down over 1,500 passengers and crew.

It had taken over three years to build the 882-foot-long Titanic. The ship offered every possible luxury for the traveler:

grand staterooms, a heated pool—even electric elevators. The design for the ship was considered so safe, most people thought the Titanic was unsinkable. They were wrong. The confidence in the ship may have caused its tragic end. Though crewmen received six warnings of iceberg sightings, the Titanic was still moving at nearly full speed when it hit the floating ice that crippled it. In a matter of hours, the giant liner had broken in two and sunk to the bottom of the ocean.

Though twenty lifeboats and a few rafts were available, there were not nearly enough spaces for the large number of people on the Titanic. An untrained crew meant that even these few boats were not filled. The water in the North Atlantic was so cold, no one could survive in it for more than a few minutes. Of the 2,227 people onboard, only 705 survived.

One of them was a wealthy woman named Margaret "Molly" Brown. She was a passenger in a lifeboat filled with women. The boat, Number 6, was commanded by one of the Titanic's officers, Robert Hichens. As the Titanic sank, Hichens kept shouting at the women to row harder, while refusing to help row himself. Molly Brown became so angry she took over command of the boat. She and her passengers managed to survive the next cold dark hours, waiting to be rescued. For her efforts, she earned the name "Unsinkable Molly Brown."

For more about **Water Transportation GO TO PAGE 132**

Boats/Ships▸Rowing

AT ONE TIME, even huge ships were human-powered by dozens of rowers. But today only small boats, such as canoes, are moved with oars and paddles. These are often simple boats with one or two passengers.

A simple paddling or rowing action pushes water back. In reaction, the boat is pushed forward. Oars and paddles are used to steer the boat, too.

Though most rowing boats move quite slowly, groups of rowers compete in races, reaching speeds of nearly 14 miles per hour. And whitewater kayaks can race along through river rapids.

Rowing boats were made from wood or animal skins until the 20th century. Though these materials are still used, metal and fiberglass began to replace natural materials in the 1960s. Since that time, molded plastic and lightweight layered materials called composites have been used to build many rowing boats.

▲ **Gondolas**
The city of Venice, Italy, is built on canals. Powered boats provide most transportation, but people sometimes still use old-fashioned boats called gondolas to travel the canals. Gondolas are propelled with one oar called a scull that is twisted as it pushes through the water.

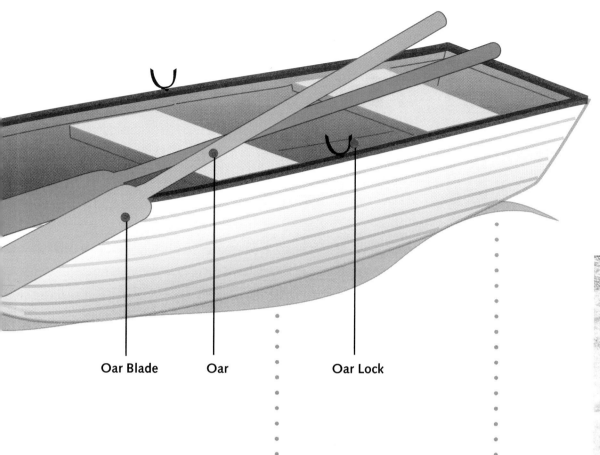

Oar Blade   Oar   Oar Lock

▼ **Whitewater Kayak**

This kayaker uses all his skill to ride the rapids. Modern kayaks are sometimes strengthened with spider silk, a material tougher than steel.

A LOOK INTO HISTORY: *The Viking Ships*

Long before Christopher Columbus crossed the Atlantic Ocean, the Vikings had been to North America. In fact, scientists have discovered scraps of tools and jewelry that prove the Vikings were in North America around 1000 A.D.

The Vikings lived in Scandinavia in Northern Europe. They built great long boats for warfare, some of which used 50 rowers, as well as smaller trading boats. In these craft they traveled all over Northern Europe. Eventually they made it all the way to North America. In their travels, Viking warriors often attacked people where they landed and stole their animals and anything else of value. Better-mannered Vikings traded things like furs and pottery. The Vikings loved decorating their boats and furnishings. Their ornaments and a few of their ships are kept in museums in Norway and Denmark.

During the 1960s, groups of Danish Boy Scouts decided to try building some Viking ships. One of their ships, the Sebbe Also, participated in Operation Sail in the United States in 1976.

For more about Water Transportation GO TO PAGE 132

Boats/Ships ▶ Sailing

IF YOU have ever tried to hold onto an umbrella on a windy day, you've felt the power of a sail. Square sails were first attached regularly to boats by the early Romans and Egyptians.

Centuries later, merchants began using triangular sails. This design worked much better than square sails, especially when several sails were used. People were now able to travel great distances on water— eventually around the world.

Sailboats are used today mainly for pleasure boating. But in the last decade, improved designs have made sail travel much faster. Double-hulled (catamaran) and triple-hulled (trimaran) boats have set many speed records. New materials keep the boats very lightweight. In the 1990s a trimaran traveled around the world in less than 80 days.

Since wind is a natural, readily available resource, new designs for rigid (hard) sails are being tested on some ships. Using more wind power would reduce the need for other fuels.

▲ **Computer Sail**
The cruise ship *Wind Song* uses rigid sails that are "trimmed" or set by a computer.

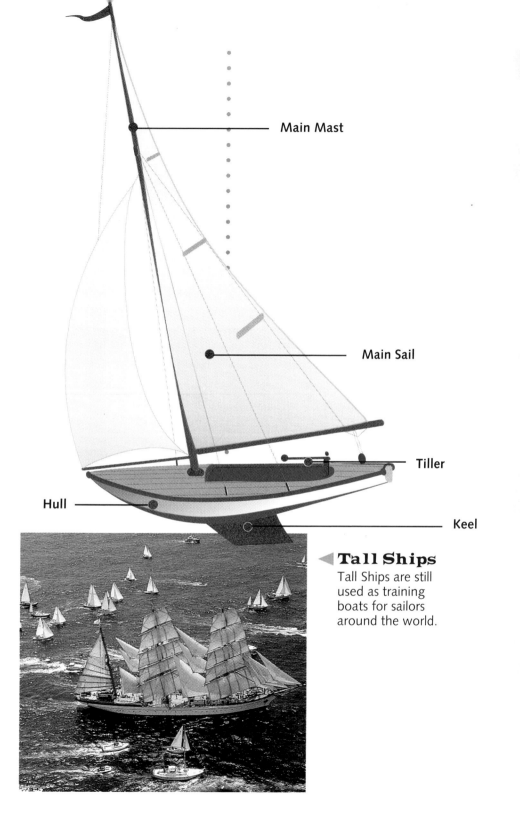

Main Mast

Main Sail

Tiller

Hull

Keel

◀ Tall Ships

Tall Ships are still used as training boats for sailors around the world.

A LOOK INTO HISTORY:
The Clipper Ships

The clipper ships were some of the fastest wind-powered boats ever to set sail, but they ruled the seas for only about ten years.

When gold was discovered in California in 1848, many people were anxious to try their luck digging for it. But the overland route from the East to California was long and dangerous. A traveler could easily die in the desert or be killed by Indians at war with the United States government. Even gold wasn't enough of a prize for most people to risk that fate.

The other way to go to California was by ship and this choice proved more popular. Giant, swift clipper ships were built in great numbers. They were designed to carry passengers from the Atlantic coast of the U.S. around South America to California.

These ships had fierce sounding names like Stag-Hound, Lightning, and Sea Witch. And they set record after record for sailing speed. Some of these records were broken only at the end of the 20th century.

Clipper captains were all men, but sometimes they sailed with their wives. Mary Ann Patten was the wife of the captain of Neptune's Car. As the ship was rounding the tip of South America, it entered a howling storm. At the same time, Captain Patten was stricken with a terrible fever. With no available second-in-command, Patten's 19-year-old wife, Mary Ann, took control. She nursed her husband and brought the ship into its California port 20 days ahead of schedule. The company that owned the ship was so grateful it collected a bonus of over $1,000 to give to Mrs. Patten.

The clipper ships died out because merchants no longer wanted to pay for the large crews needed to sail them. In a dozen years the lovely swift clipper was gone from the sea. But it still holds a place in history—a lasting symbol of the beauty and power of sail.

For more about
Water Transportation
GO TO PAGE 132

Boats/Ships ▸ Sailing Designs

SAILBOATS are rigged, or fitted, with sails. They may have one or more masts and different numbers, shapes, and sizes of sails. These are some traditional designs for sailing boats.

Schooner

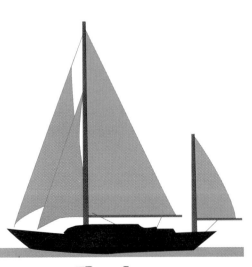

Yawl

Brig

Full-Rigged Ship

Bark

Ketch

Catboat

Sloop

Cutter

Boats/Ships▸Working

MANY SHIPS AND BOATS are built to do special jobs in the water. Here are some craft that are working hard in waterways around the world.

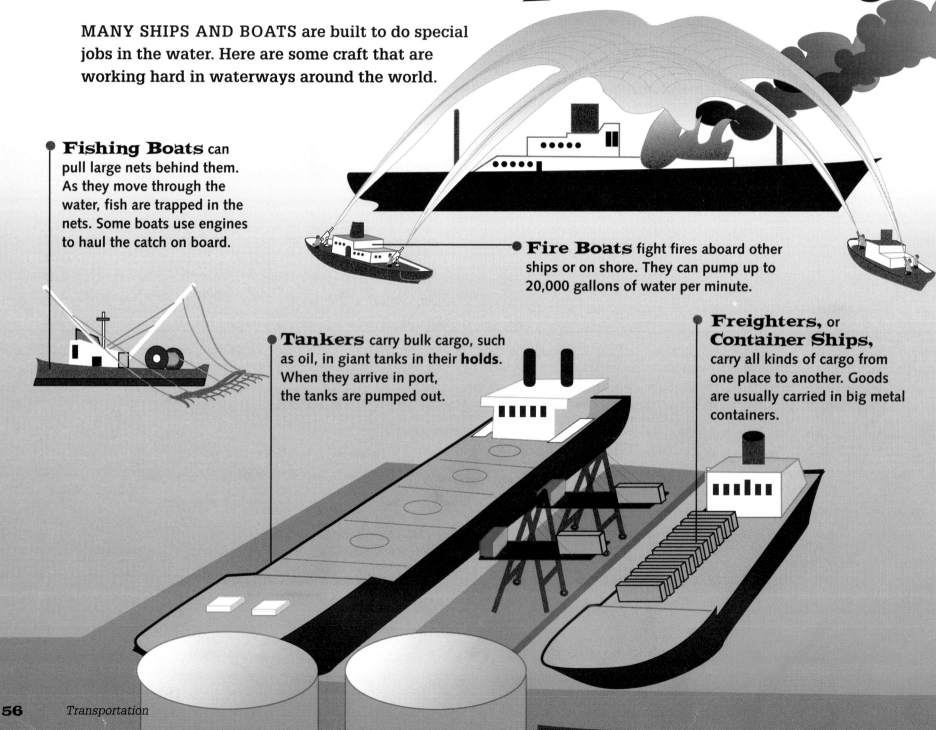

Fishing Boats can pull large nets behind them. As they move through the water, fish are trapped in the nets. Some boats use engines to haul the catch on board.

Fire Boats fight fires aboard other ships or on shore. They can pump up to 20,000 gallons of water per minute.

Tankers carry bulk cargo, such as oil, in giant tanks in their **holds**. When they arrive in port, the tanks are pumped out.

Freighters, or **Container Ships,** carry all kinds of cargo from one place to another. Goods are usually carried in big metal containers.

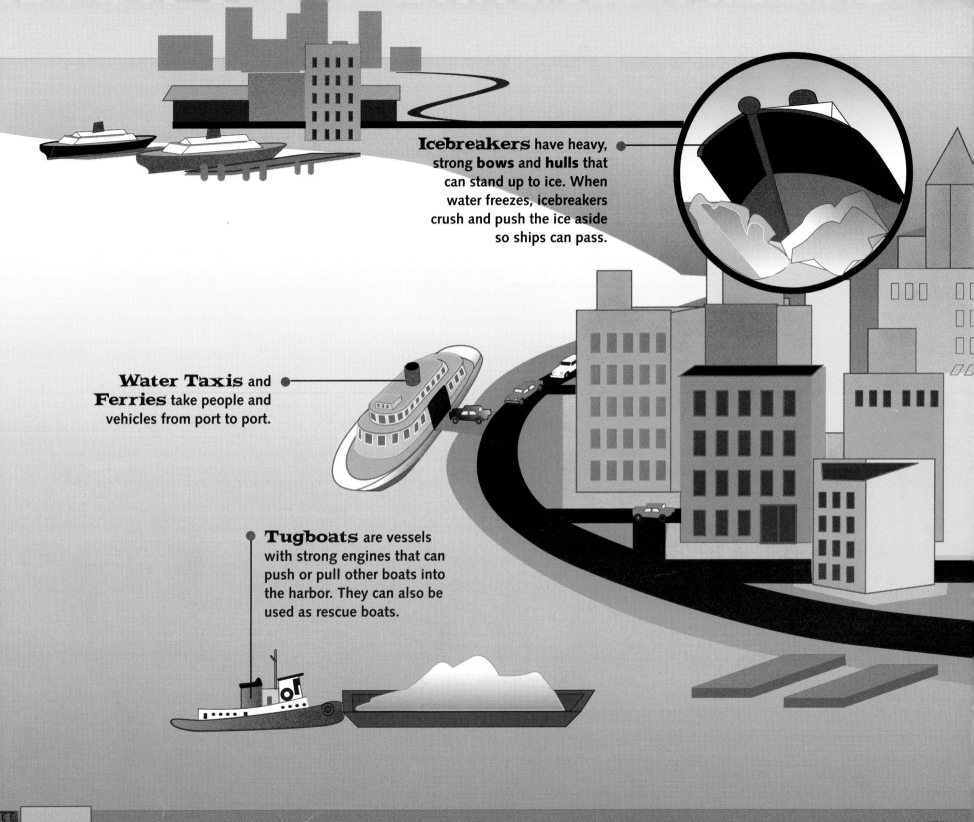

Icebreakers have heavy, strong **bows** and **hulls** that can stand up to ice. When water freezes, icebreakers crush and push the ice aside so ships can pass.

Water Taxis and **Ferries** take people and vehicles from port to port.

Tugboats are vessels with strong engines that can push or pull other boats into the harbor. They can also be used as rescue boats.

Bridges

IF YOU have ever needed to cross some water and didn't have a boat, you understand why people invented bridges. Bridges let people and vehicles travel over water or sharp dips in the land. The lengths of bridges can vary from several feet to several miles.

To build a bridge, engineers must think about how long and wide the bridge needs to be and where and how the supports will be placed. They also must consider the traffic flow—the number of vehicles that will pass over the bridge. The height and width of any vehicles that may move under the bridge are also important.

Many different materials are used to build bridges including rope, wood, stone, concrete, and steel.

Bridge builders use many different structures to support, or hold up, a bridge's span. These spans are the roadways or walkways that vehicles or people cross. Builders may choose different kinds of supports, such as arches or cables, to keep bridges strong and steady. Some bridges, called drawbridges, swing or lift part of their span to let ships pass.

The Golden Gate Bridge
Ten thousand tons of steel and 80,000 miles of wire cable went into building the Golden Gate Bridge. Constructed in 1937, the bridge span stretches 4,260 feet. It's one of the tallest bridges in the world.

◄ **Vertical Stay Bridges**

The Sunset Skyway in Florida is an example of a stay bridge. The cables that support the bridge's span are attached directly to it.

▶ **The Brooklyn Bridge**

The suspension bridge over New York's East River is more than 100 years old. It is one of over 2,000 bridges in New York City.

Supports

Span

A LOOK INTO HISTORY: *Building the Brooklyn Bridge*

One of the most exciting building projects during the late 1800s was the suspension bridge *being built in New York City.* When finished, it would span the East River, between Brooklyn and Manhattan. It would be the longest suspension bridge in the world.

John Roebling designed the bridge, and his son Washington was hired to build it. Because the bridge span was so long, the towers it was attached to had to be buried deep under the water. As the towers were being placed, many workers were stricken with the "bends." This is a disease brought on by staying under deep water and coming up too quickly. Washington Roebling himself fell so sick, he could no longer

work on the bridge. The Brooklyn Bridge would have never been completed had it not been for Washington's wife, Emily.

Emily Roebling was a quiet person, but she took over for her husband. For more than a dozen years she supervised the bridge's construction. She dealt with the builders, suppliers, and the politicians who were eager to see the project finished.

Today there are longer suspension bridges in the world. But nearly all of them owe much of their design to the Brooklyn Bridge—and the efforts of the Roebling family.

For more about Land Transportation GO TO PAGE 86

Bridges ▸ Designs

SIMPLE BRIDGES use a single span, or roadway, with supports. But many other bridges have more complicated designs. These are some of the kinds of bridges you might see when you travel.

The curved shape of an **Arch Bridge** lets the weight of the bridge span rest on side supports. These can be made of many kinds of materials, including stone and concrete.

The span of a **Suspension Bridge** hangs, or is suspended, from large steel cables that are draped over the bridge's towers. The cables are attached to blocks of concrete at both ends of the bridge.

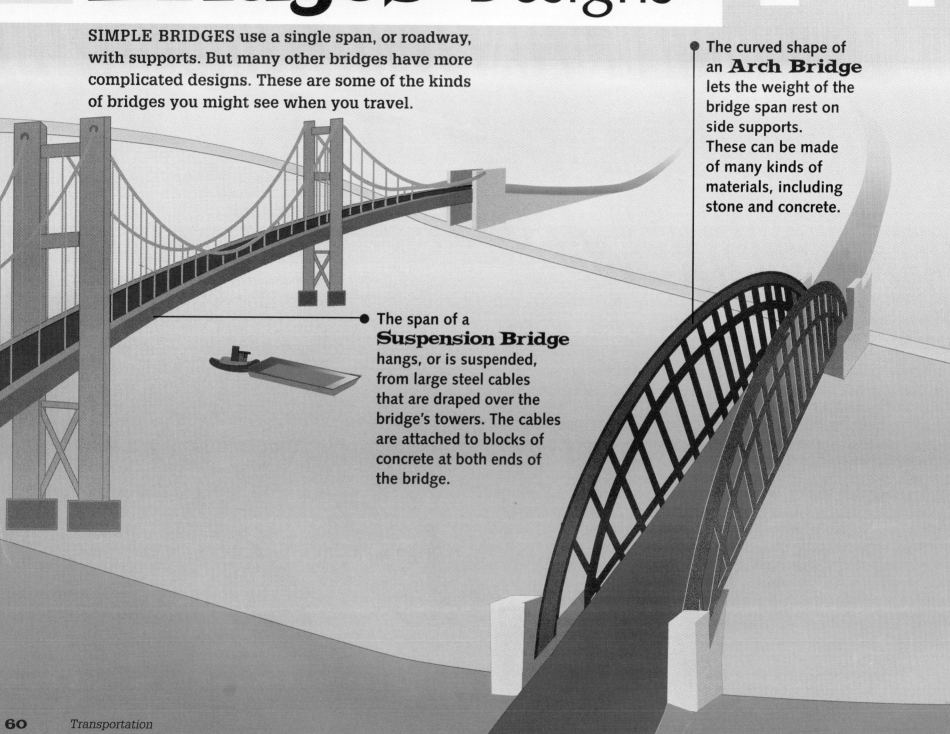

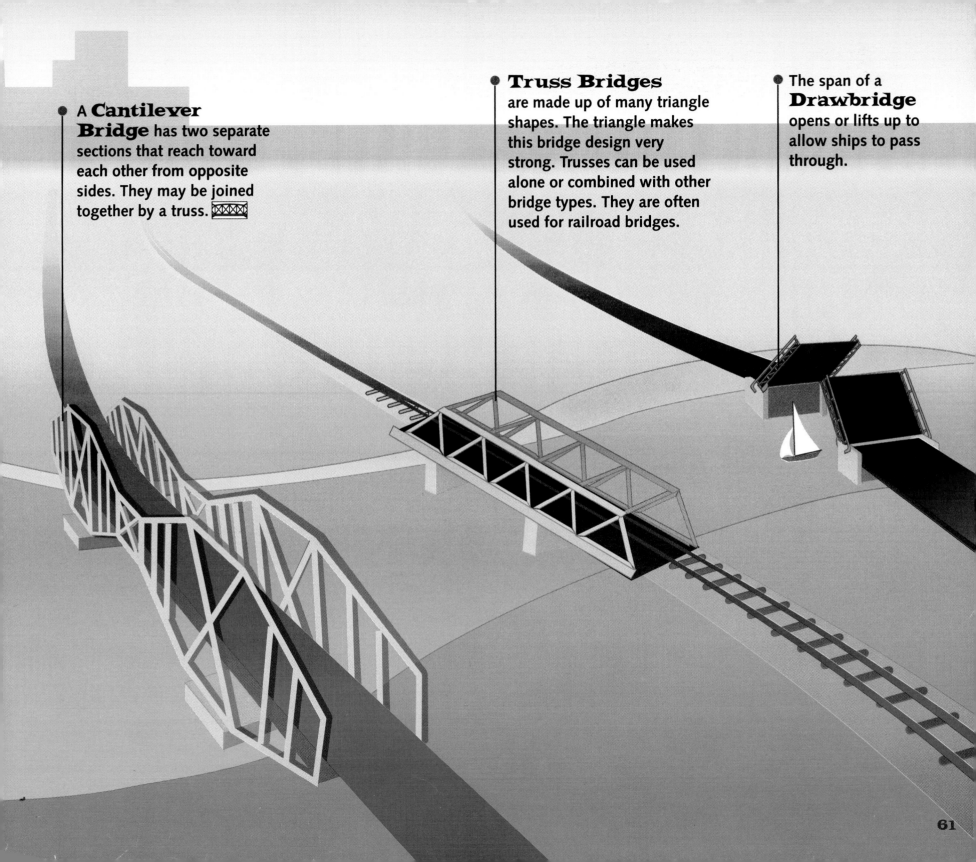

A **Cantilever Bridge** has two separate sections that reach toward each other from opposite sides. They may be joined together by a truss.

Truss Bridges are made up of many triangle shapes. The triangle makes this bridge design very strong. Trusses can be used alone or combined with other bridge types. They are often used for railroad bridges.

The span of a **Drawbridge** opens or lifts up to allow ships to pass through.

Buses

BUSES are used by millions of people to travel to school, work, and other places. In the United States, they are the most popular form of public transportation. Large buses can carry up to 70 people and are less expensive to operate than trains or planes.

Although they look a bit different, buses are really trucks in disguise. In fact, for many years buses were designed and built by the companies that made heavy-duty trucks.

Instead of an empty frame, buses have seats for many passengers and a lower floor than trucks have. Wide windows, sometimes fitted with shaded glass, let people see outside as they ride. Large buses often use air pressure to open and shut doors and operate other working parts. Many modern city buses can "kneel" so that people with disabilities can get on and off easily. Others have steps that drop for wheelchairs and walkers. Nearly all buses have diesel engines.

Aerodynamic buses can save as much as 25 percent on fuel, so new bus designs are sleeker with rounded edges. Some large buses are articulated, or separated into different sections like some trucks. In fact some modern bus designs actually use a truck-like cab that is separate from the passenger section. Different size trailers fitted with seats can be attached to the same bus tractor.

Rural Bus Service

Some buses, like this one in Pakistan, may be the only form of group transportation available. They are used to carry nearly everything, including bicycles and livestock.

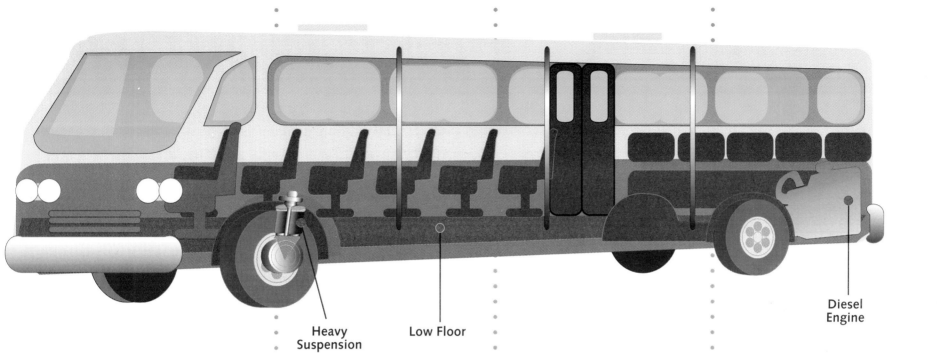

Heavy
Suspension

Low Floor

Diesel
Engine

◀ **Passenger Bus**

Because they don't need
tracks like trains or subways,
buses are a handy form of
public transportation. This
bus on the streets of London,
England, is a double-decker
that carries passengers on
two levels. A stairway allows
people to pass from one
level to the other.

**For more about
Land Transportation
GO TO PAGE 86**

Canals

CANALS are human-made waterways that usually connect two natural bodies of water. The basic idea of a canal is to create a connecting waterway through land so boats can pass easily. Otherwise, they would have to travel much further to find a natural water passage.

Canals have been used for more than 2,000 years. Many of the canals built during the 19th and 20th centuries are true wonders. Builders carved waterhighways hundreds of miles long, sometimes cutting through massive stone and earth barriers.

Often the path a canal will follow is not level.

Mountains, hills, or deep valleys cause big problems for boats moving across them. Engineers must use different methods to keep boats moving smoothly. Where one section of water level is much higher than another, locks with gates are used. These are a kind of water elevator or stairway that helps ships move up and down—from one water level to another.

It's also important that the water is deep enough throughout the route of the canal. Often feeder canals are run into the main canal to add water when it's needed. Dredger boats remove excess mud and sand from the waterway to keep it clear.

▲ **Suez Canal**
The Suez Canal connects the Mediterranean with the Red Sea.
The canal is 103 miles long.

LOCK

Gate

A LOOK INTO HISTORY: *Building the Panama Canal*

▲ **Panama Canal**
Electric trains are used to pull ships through the Miraflores Locks.

If you had mentioned the Panama Canal to almost anyone in 1891, they probably would have laughed at you. At the end of the 19th century, most people thought this new canal was a giant joke.

The French government had been trying to build the waterway for nine years. But they had met with disaster after disaster.

At first glance, the waterway seemed like a great idea. To travel from New York to San Francisco, boats had to sail down the Atlantic coast of North and South America and back up the Pacific coast. The canal cut a 40-mile-long path through Central America. This shortcut would reduce the Atlantic-to-Pacific voyage by 9,000 miles.

But the Panama Canal ended up being more trouble than people bargained for. The ground where the canal was being dug was soft and kept sliding. Twenty thousand workers died of malaria and other tropical diseases. Eventually the French gave up.

In 1903, after a war with Colombia, the United States took over the building of the canal. Army doctors discovered that the malaria virus was carried by mosquitoes, so they set about controlling the insect. For the next eleven years, in steaming heat, thousands of workers carved out the waterway.

More than 61 million pounds of dynamite were used to slice through the mountains. Workers built six huge locks, which raised and lowered the water so ships could pass from one level to another.

In 1914, the canal was officially opened. The total job had taken more than 30 years. Thousands of workers had died and hundreds of millions of dollars were spent. But the canal is still at work. It is a real tribute to the people who managed to do what most people thought was impossible.

For more about Water Transportation GO TO PAGE 132

Carriages, Carts, and Buggies

Amish Cart
Many Amish people in Pennsylvania, Ohio, and other areas shun automobiles. All of their vehicles are horse-drawn.

ANIMAL-DRAWN CARRIAGES, carts, and buggies served as the main personal vehicles until cars were invented. For centuries, taxis, ambulances, buses, and most other vehicles were pulled by animals.

When the gasoline-powered automobile was invented, it shared the streets with these older types of vehicles. As the popularity of cars increased, though, carts and carriages were forced off the road in most cities and towns.

In the 1940s, gasoline supplies were short because of World War II. Once again, people hauled out their old carriages. Horse-drawn vehicles didn't require gasoline and they provided reliable transportation. At the same time, people were once again reminded of the pleasure of riding in carriages. After the war, people returned to their automobiles, but interest in horse-drawn vehicles has continued.

Today carts and wagons are still used in rural areas in many countries. Many cities now provide carriage rides for tourists, while horse-drawn racers compete on tracks around the world.

Carriages and carts may be pulled by one or more animals. The animal is attached to the vehicle by wooden or metal poles or shafts, and straps of rope or leather.

The driver controls the animals with reins which are connected to the animal's head and body.

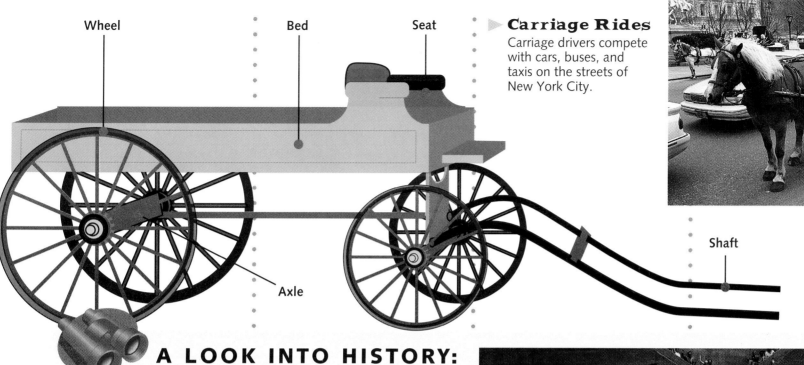

Wheel   Bed   Seat

Axle

Shaft

Carriage Rides
Carriage drivers compete with cars, buses, and taxis on the streets of New York City.

A LOOK INTO HISTORY:
Roman Wheels

Many types of wheeled carts and other vehicles have been used since ancient times. The Egyptians, Greeks, and Romans all used chariots for hunting, traveling, and racing. The Romans, who had an excellent system of roads, created many different vehicles to drive on them.

Roman men used a special chariot, called a currus for travel in cities. Though this chariot was popular, it was not exactly comfortable. The driver had no seat and had to stand as he handled the animals pulling the vehicle. Roman women were luckier. Their somewhat lighter cart, called a monachus, had a seat. It could be pulled by a single horse or mule. Women in pairs rode in an enclosed cart called a carpentum.

For larger groups of people, a vehicle called a rheda had seats for six passengers. Usually pulled by oxen, these carriages were sometimes used as taxis. The Romans also had a variety of working vehicles including mail carts, farm vehicles, and ambulances.

After the end of the Roman Empire, chariots gradually fell out of favor. In fact, for centuries in Europe, it was considered undignified for men to ride on wheels at all. By the late 1500s,

Chariots
Charlton Heston rides a Roman war chariot in the movie, *Ben Hur.*

though, wheeled vehicles once again returned to the streets. The French King Henri IV took it upon himself to rid his countrymen of the taboo against wheels. He took great pleasure speeding through Paris in his elegant, curtained carrosse— until he was killed in it.

For more about Land Transportation GO TO PAGE 86

Elevators

ELEVATORS are basically lifting machines. They use a pulley–a wheel with a cable–and a weight to move their loads up and down. Elevators almost always run on electricity. They have carefully designed braking systems that keep them from falling—even if a cable breaks.

While most people use elevators to get to upper floors in tall buildings, elevators also move people under the earth's surface. Parking garages, subways, and mines all use elevators to lower people under the ground.

One of the more unusual ideas for a lifting machine is the "space elevator." This elevator would be attached with a tether to a satellite circling the earth. It would carry people and materials back and forth from space much less expensively than spaceships. The space elevator is not realistic now, but might appear in the future. Scientists have already experimented with tethered satellites connected to the Space Shuttle.

Most earthbound elevators move at about five miles per hour. But some elevators can travel ten times that speed. Though individual elevator trips are short, elevators do travel great distances. The average elevator in New York City travels about 10,000 miles each year.

Elevator Design
Glass elevators add elegance to buildings. They have a practical benefit, too—passengers can see the environment around them as they go up and down.

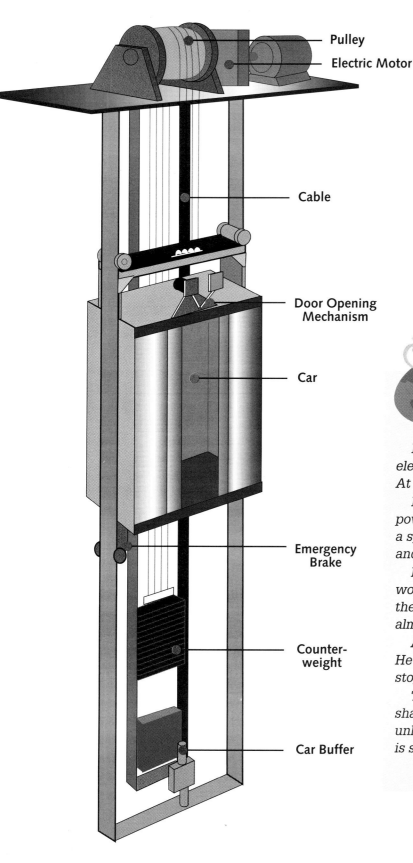

Pulley

Electric Motor

Cable

Door Opening
Mechanism

Car

Emergency
Brake

Counter-
weight

Car Buffer

TRANSPORATION FIRST:
The Safety Elevator

In the 17th and 18th centuries, people started to use simple freight elevators (flying chairs and dumbwaiters) to carry heavy loads between floors. At this time, no one was using elevators to carry people. It seemed too risky.

But a man named Elisha Otis changed all that. In 1852, he invented a steam-powered elevator—with a difference. Otis's elevator had two metal hooks and a spring. If a cable failed, the hooks sprang out. They caught onto guide rails and stopped the elevator from falling.

Reportedly, Otis proved the safety of his elevator in a startling way. He would climb aboard an elevator platform in front of an audience. When he had their attention, his assistant would cut the cable. Otis's fall would be stopped almost instantly by the safety hooks.

An African-American inventor, Alexander Miles, made elevators even safer. He found a way to close up the shaft above and below the elevator when it stopped. This kept the car from moving when people were getting on and off.

Today most elevators also have a buffer, or cushion, at the bottom of the shaft. This provides extra protection in case the elevator does fall. But that's unlikely. Statistics show that riding an elevator is safer than using the stairs.

For more about Land Transportation GO TO PAGE 86

Engines

ENGINES use fuel to create the form of energy that a vehicle needs to move. Here are some of the basic engines used in transportation.

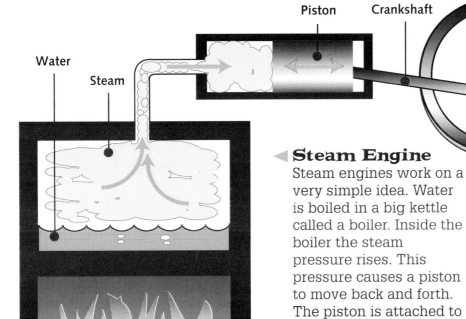

Water

Steam

Piston

Crankshaft

◀ Steam Engine

Steam engines work on a very simple idea. Water is boiled in a big kettle called a boiler. Inside the boiler the steam pressure rises. This pressure causes a piston to move back and forth. The piston is attached to a crankshaft. The crankshaft turns the up-and-down motion into a rotary, or circling motion. Steam engines are still used on steam trains.

▽ In a **Steam Turbine Engine**, the steam from the boiler blows against something like a windmill. This "windmill" rotates a shaft. Steam turbines are very powerful engines. Steam turbine engines are used to power large ships like aircraft carriers.

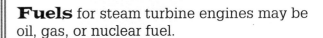

Rotating Shaft

Fuels for steam engines in trains can be coal or wood.

Fuels for steam turbine engines may be oil, gas, or nuclear fuel.

Internal Combustion Engine

Gasoline and diesel engines are known as internal combustion engines. This means the fuel is set on fire right inside the engine. The energy from the expanding fuel mixture moves the piston directly. Internal combustion engines are used in many vehicles including cars, trucks, and some aircraft.

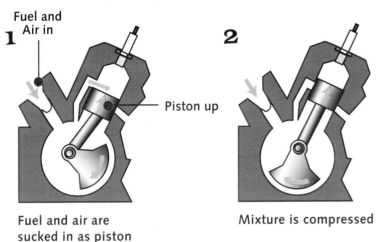

1 Fuel and Air in

Fuel and air are sucked in as piston moves up

2 Piston up

Mixture is compressed

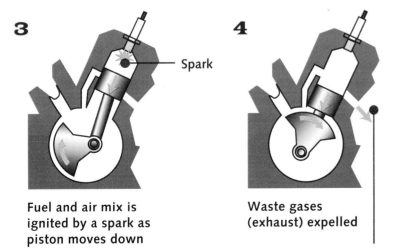

3 Spark

Fuel and air mix is ignited by a spark as piston moves down

4

Waste gases (exhaust) expelled

Waste Gas out

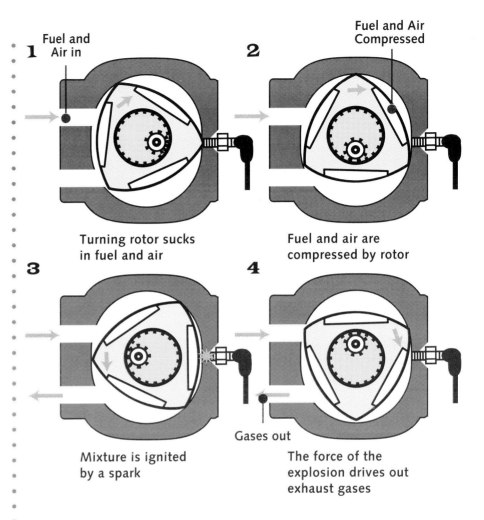

1 Fuel and Air in

Turning rotor sucks in fuel and air

2 Fuel and Air Compressed

Fuel and air are compressed by rotor

3

Mixture is ignited by a spark

4

Gases out

The force of the explosion drives out exhaust gases

Rotary Engines are internal combustion engines, too. But instead of causing an up-and-down movement, they cause a turning, or circular, movement. Rotary engines are used to turn propellers in aircraft and boats.

Fuels for internal combustion engines may be gasoline, diesel, propane or natural gas, alcohol, and others.

71

Engines

GAS TURBINE engines combine the features of the internal combustion engine with the steam turbine. Instead of steam, the pressure of burning fuel rotates a turbine.

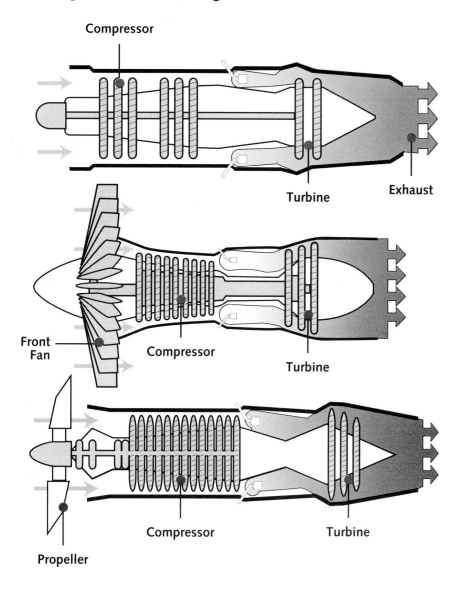

Compressor

Turbine   Exhaust

Front Fan   Compressor

Turbine

Propeller

Compressor   Turbine

Turbojets use a compressor to pull in air and squeeze, or compress, it. Fuel is sprayed into the intake air, then ignited, making it expand. The hot gases move past a turbine, turning it. They are then forced out the back of the engine.

Turbojets are used in supersonic planes, such as jet fighters and the *Concorde*.

Turbofan engines are similar to turbojet engines, but they are quieter and less expensive to run. In a turbofan, some of the air pulled in the engine is used to cool and quiet it. This extra air, when it exits the engine, helps to provide power at low speeds.

Turbofan engines are used in most jet airplanes.

In a **Turboprop engine**, hot, compressed gases are used to drive a propeller.

Turboprop engines are used by many small aircraft including airships. They are also used in some boats.

Fuels for gas turbine engines are mainly gas, alcohol, or diesel. Jet airplanes use a fuel formula called JP4. It's similar to kerosene.

▶ Rockets

Rocket engines work by burning fuel in a tube or chamber. The hot gases expand and rush out the open end. Rockets that are used in space usually have separate tanks containing liquid fuel and liquid oxygen. These two liquids are fed into a combustion chamber as power is needed.

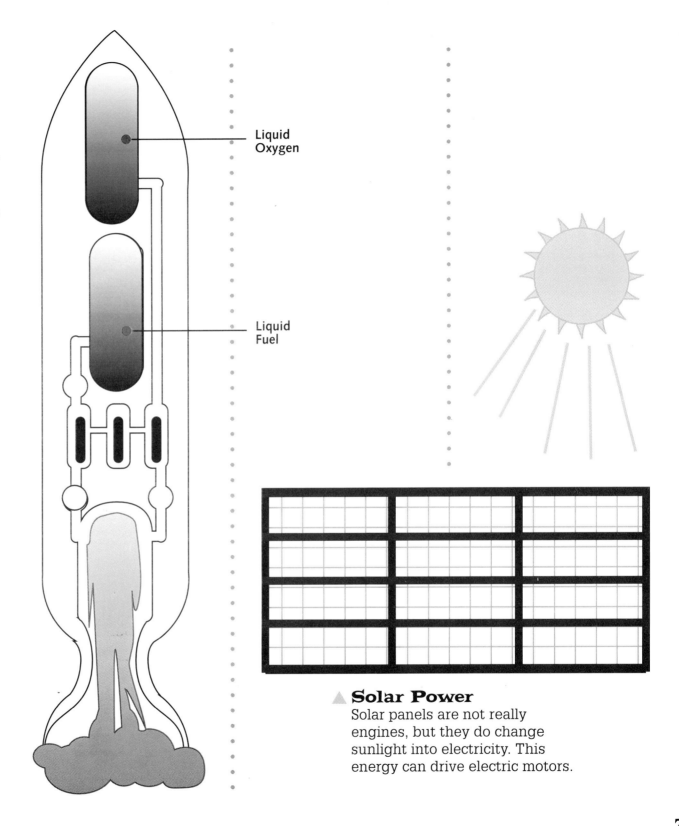

Liquid Oxygen

Liquid Fuel

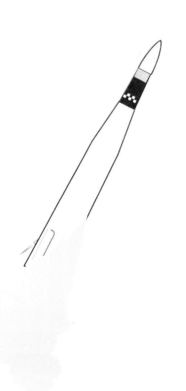

▲ Solar Power

Solar panels are not really engines, but they do change sunlight into electricity. This energy can drive electric motors.

Escalators

AS YOU STEP on an escalator, the steps magically appear. When you get off, they magically disappear. If you could look inside the escalator, you'd see the work going on behind the magic. An escalator is really an endless belt. As the stairs fold flat at the top, they go around a big wheel and then return to the bottom of the stairway. There they go around another wheel that rolls the steps back up.

Escalators are used in multistoried buildings, in subways, airports, and other public areas. They are especially useful in places where people move a lot between connecting floors. In malls and department stores, for example, people riding a slow-moving escalator can look around as they go up or down.

An electric motor powers the escalator. Rubber or plastic moving handrails and steps with grooved treads help people to ride escalators safely. These moving steps usually travel about 100 feet per minute.

Longest Ride
The world's tallest bank of escalators is in London, England.

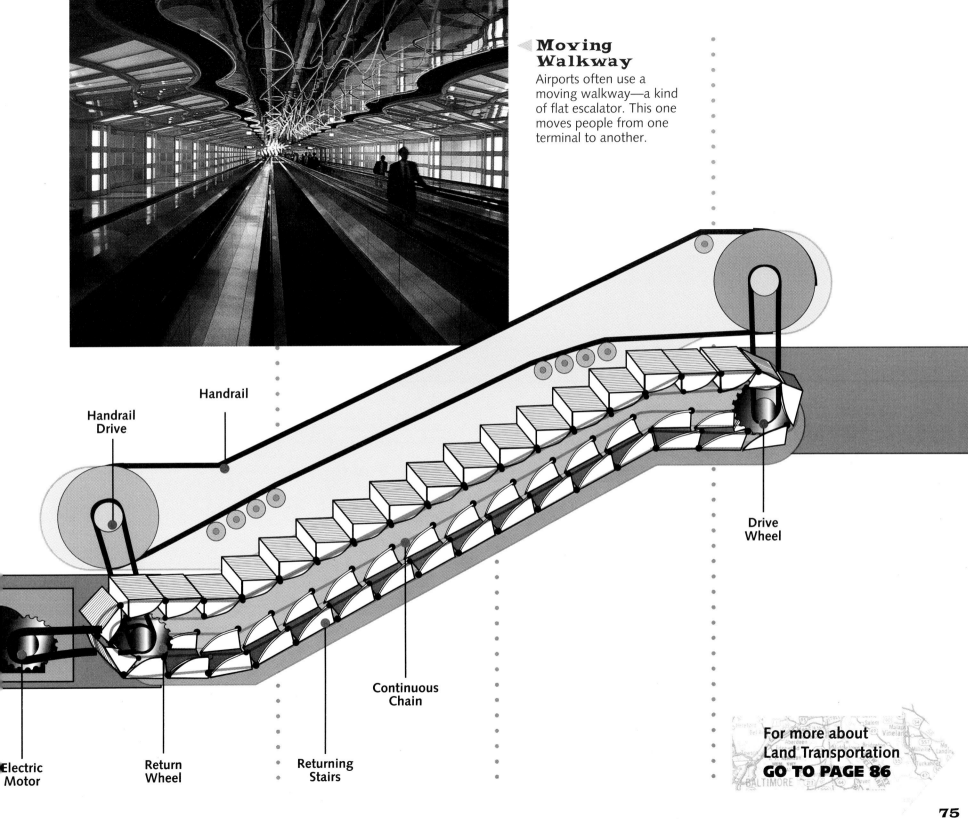

Moving Walkway

Airports often use a moving walkway—a kind of flat escalator. This one moves people from one terminal to another.

Handrail

Handrail Drive

Drive Wheel

Electric Motor

Return Wheel

Returning Stairs

Continuous Chain

For more about
Land Transportation
GO TO PAGE 86

Foot Travel

WHILE FEET aren't exactly a vehicle, they do provide a form of transportation—walking. Walking and running are efficient ways of getting around, not to mention good exercise. A person on foot doesn't cause air pollution or traffic jams.

The only thing you really need for walking is a pair of feet and working leg muscles. In a single day, an average person will walk between five and ten miles. That's more than 180,000 miles—about five trips around the world—in an average lifetime.

The bones in your foot move apart a little bit every time you step down. This helps spread out the shock of your weight. Still, if you're not walking on soft ground like dirt or sand, most feet require a little protection. Shoes help to support the feet and keep them from getting hurt.

Modern sneakers and walking shoes are specially designed to keep your feet safe and comfortable. Special shoes with cleats or spurs allow their wearers to play sports or walk on difficult surfaces.

Ice Climbing
Using shoes with spikes, an ice climber works his way through a crevice in the Arctic. Footwear can be adapted in many ways. Wheels, blades, webbing, or cleats allow the foot to move easily on a variety of surfaces.

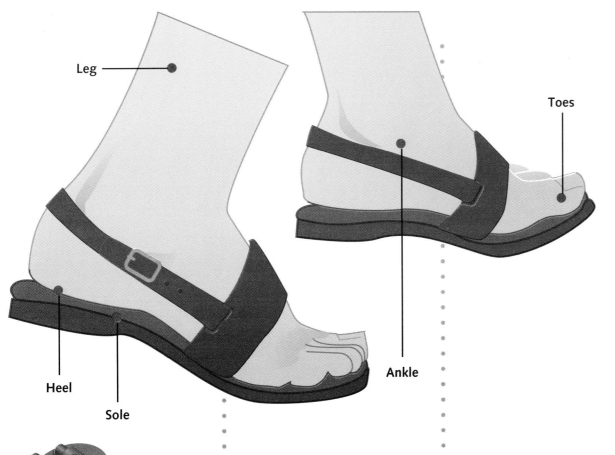

Leg

Toes

Heel

Sole

Ankle

▲ Rolling Along
Wheels add speed to your feet. One in-line design features a model plane engine attached to the skate.

A LOOK INTO HISTORY: *The Oregon Trail*

Hundreds of thousands of American pioneers trod the Oregon Trail (from Missouri to Oregon) in the years 1843 to 1860—a 2,000-mile trek. Many walked the entire way, using their animals to carry belongings. Oregon Trail walkers were called Overlanders because many others were sailing on clipper ships to the West around the tip of South America. The overland journey was hard—the survivors suffered through droughts, raids, and wild animal attacks. But their footpaths opened the way to the West for thousands of European settlers.

◀ Long Distance Walkers
Traffic over the Oregon Trail left ruts in the land that are still visible today.

For more about Land Transportation GO TO PAGE 86

Harbors

HARBORS OR PORTS are places where ships and boats come in to dock, like big parking lots for cars. Like airports, harbors come in a variety of sizes. Here are some of the features found in a large port or harbor.

Ships move in and out using water roadways known as **Channels**. There are strict rules about speed and passing, just as there are for cars on roads.

Ships are parked in deep-water **Roads** while they wait for **Dock Space**.

Long Wharves provide places for workers to load or unload cargo. Some cargo may be stored in **Warehouses**.

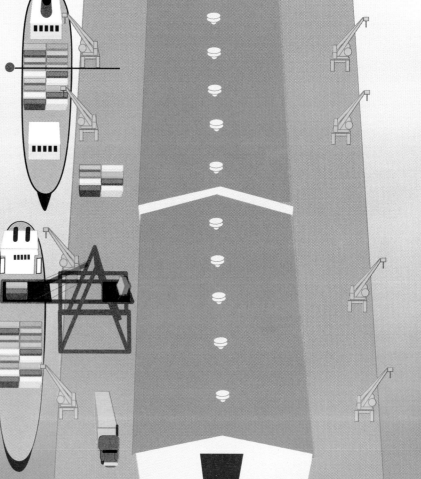

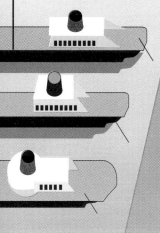

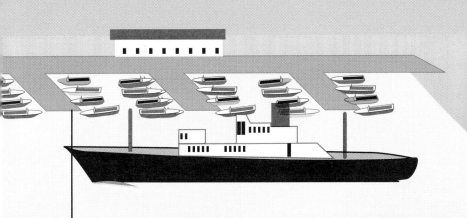

buoy

beacon

Buoys, Lights, and **Beacons** are used to direct ship traffic. **Radar** (radio waves) is used for traffic control.

Pleasure boats are docked, or parked, at **Marinas**.

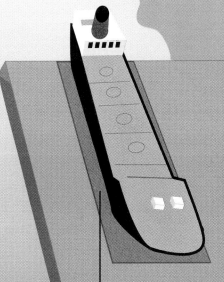

In **Dry Docks**, a boat's hull, or bottom, can be serviced or repaired. Chemicals or paint are applied to keep ocean plants and creatures from attaching themselves to the ship.

Helicopters

BECAUSE it can fly and land practically anywhere, the helicopter is excellent for military or rescue missions. It can be used in remote areas, such as canyons, or on mountains where it would be impossible to land an airplane.

Lightweight but powerful engines turn the rotors of the helicopter, lifting it into the air. By angling the rotor and its blades, the pilot can move the aircraft in any direction—forward, backward, or to the side. A tail rotor keeps the "chopper" stable. Because rotors, not fixed wings, are used for lift, a chopper can move straight up or straight down. It can even hover over one spot as long as its fuel lasts. Most medium and large helicopters now use jet engines. Smaller helicopters are still powered by gasoline engines.

Like many other aircraft, helicopters now contain lightweight composite materials. Some military choppers are built with kevlar, the material used in bulletproof vests. This fiber, which is five times stronger than steel, keeps them from being penetrated by enemy fire.

Helicopter designers continue to look for ways to combine the advantages of helicopters with those of planes with fixed wings. The tilt-rotor is one such design. This aircraft takes off like a helicopter. The rotor then tilts to become a propeller, so the helicopter can then fly as a plane.

▲ Helicopter Rescue

The helicopter may be the ultimate rescue vehicle. It's estimated that it has saved over one million lives.

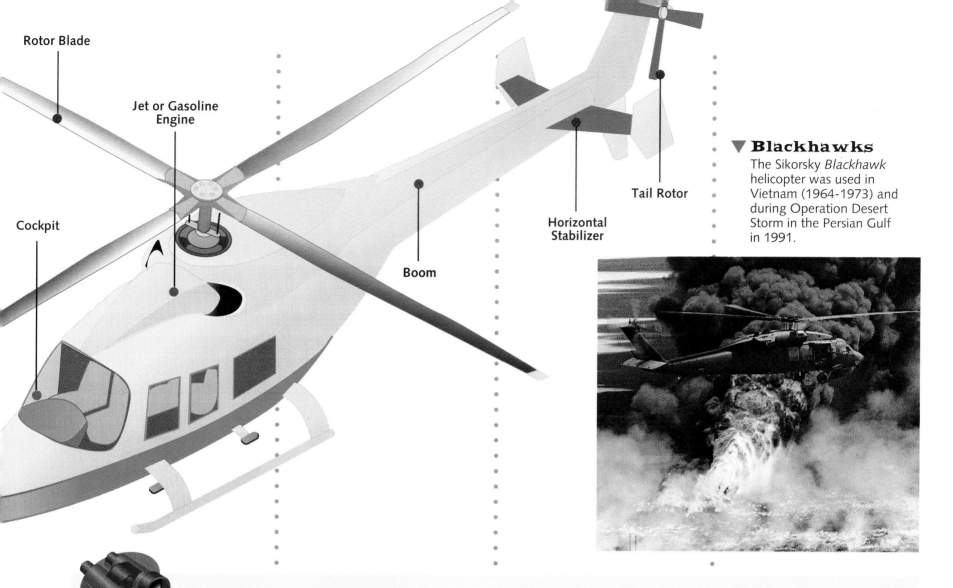

Rotor Blade

Jet or Gasoline Engine

Cockpit

Boom

Horizontal Stabilizer

Tail Rotor

▼ **Blackhawks**

The Sikorsky *Blackhawk* helicopter was used in Vietnam (1964-1973) and during Operation Desert Storm in the Persian Gulf in 1991.

A LOOK INTO HISTORY: *The Helicopter Comes of Age*

Leonardo da Vinci, an Italian artist and inventor, thought up the idea for a helicopter nearly six hundred years ago. He drew one in his notebook. Da Vinci's chopper wouldn't have worked if it had been built. (For one thing the right materials to construct it didn't exist at that time.) But da Vinci's sketch started people thinking about choppers. In the 1800s, in fact, French children—and adults—played with tiny toy helicopters.

Then in 1907, a Frenchman, Paul Cornu, built a big chopper. It did get off the ground but only for about 20 seconds.

German engineers came up with several helicopter designs in the 1930s. But it was a Russian-American, Igor Sikorsky, who patented his design for a working helicopter in 1939.

Many people didn't believe that a helicopter would be useful even if it did work. But Sikorsky believed in his idea and in time his invention was a great success. The helicopter is still one of the most useful aircraft ever built.

For more about Air Transportation **GO TO PAGE 24**

Hovercraft

A HOVERCRAFT uses compressed, or squashed, air to float over the water or land. A powerful lift-fan blows air beneath the hover's flexible skirt. This trapped air creates a cushion that the vehicle rides on. Propellers move the craft forward and from side to side. Rear fins help to steer the hover and give it stability.

The hover's ability to travel over land or water makes it useful for almost any kind of transport.

Hovers were first used for patrols and rescue work by the United States military forces in Vietnam during the 1960s. Most hovercraft are still built and used by the military. Large hovers are also providing long-distance ferry service across the English Channel between Great Britain and France, as well as in Russia and Scandinavia.

Mini-hovers are used for sports, research, crop-dusting, and fire fighting. Larger hovers have been used for rescues and ice breaking.

◄ Over Land or Water
Because they float on an air cushion, hovers can drive over very rough terrain without being damaged.

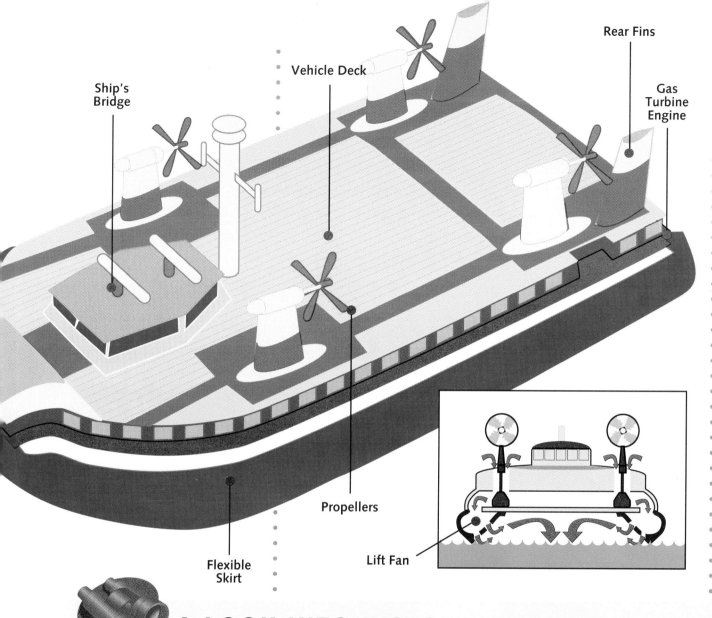

Ship's
Bridge

Vehicle Deck

Rear Fins

Gas
Turbine
Engine

Propellers

Flexible
Skirt

Lift Fan

▼ **Hover Rescue**
Hovercraft are frequently used to rescue victims in floods and other disasters.

A LOOK INTO HISTORY: *Tracking the Hovercraft*

The idea for a hovercraft goes all the way back to the mid-1800s. But as with the helicopter, the technology for building one wasn't available then. At the turn of the 20th century, several hovercraft models were put together, but none of them was very practical.

The first workable hovercraft began in 1955 with some empty tin cans and a vacuum cleaner. With the help of these household objects, the British inventor Chris Cockerell figured out how to make a practical vehicle float using trapped air. Many uses for the hovercraft have been discovered since then. And hovercraft technology, the flotation idea, has also found another home—in the design of high-speed magnetic trains.

For more about
Land Transportation
GO TO PAGE 86

Hydrofoils

USING a set of water wings, or foils, a hydrofoil actually flies through water. The wings on the hydrofoil have a curved surface at the top. When water passes over them at high speed, it causes the wings to rise in the water. The hydrofoil's hull is then lifted above the waterline.

Being above the water cuts down on the drag on the boat's hull and lets it move faster. When the hydrofoil slows down or stops, the hull settles back into the water.

Riding a hydrofoil can be a bumpy experience in rough water. But high-tech sonar helps to plot a smoother course. The hydrofoil computer uses the sonar to sense upcoming water waves. It automatically adjusts the wings of the craft to meet them.

Hydrofoils usually use turboprop engines for power. Several countries, including the United States, use these craft for military patrols. Some hydrofoils even carry guided missiles. Most others are used to ferry passengers.

◀ **Hydrofoil Action**
The foils of this hydrofoil are still below the waterline. Once the vessel picks up speed, the body or hull of the boat will lift up out of the water and ride on the foils.

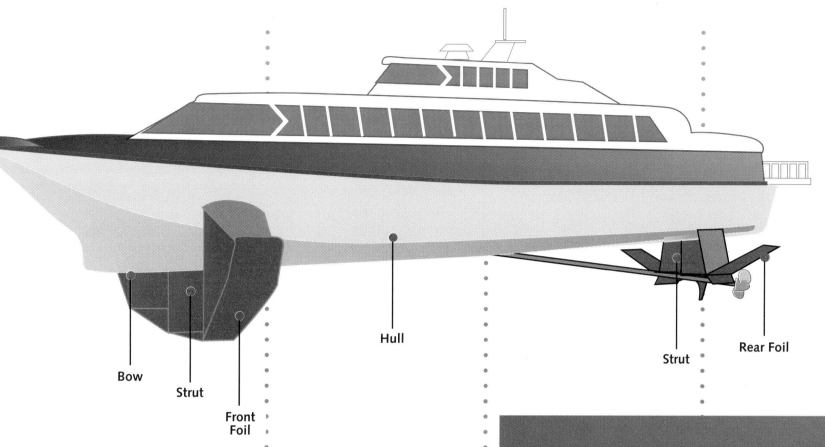

Bow

Strut

Front Foil

Hull

Strut

Rear Foil

![S] CIENCE CLOSE-UP:
How Water Foils Work

The force that causes moving air to lift a plane into the sky works in the water as well. When water moves over a foil connected to a boat, it creates more pressure underneath the foil than above it. This pressure lifts the boat up. The more it lifts up, the less drag affects it. The boat can move faster or use less energy at the same speed.

Hydrofoils are not the only boats that use foils. Racing yachts and some other boats have begun to use these water wings to increase speed.

▲ Hydrofoil Ferries

Some hydrofoil-type vehicles are now powered by water jets instead of propellers. These craft are called jet-foils.

For more about
Water Transportation
GO TO PAGE 132

Land Travel ▸ Basics

VEHICLES move across the ground in different ways. Some—like cars, bicycles, and skates—roll on wheels. Most trains use wheels, too, but they run on tracks. Skis, skates, and sleds use smooth runners to slide along the surface. Modern hovercraft and maglevs—magnetic trains—move along just above the ground.

Friction happens when things rub together. It causes resistance, making things stick and slowing things down. It also produces heat. Extreme friction stops all movement.

▸ Wheels

Wheels help reduce friction. Wheels can move on rough surfaces. But putting them on smooth roads or rails lets them move more easily and faster. It cuts down on the energy they require to move.

Wheels get into trouble, though, when the surfaces they roll on turn bumpy or muddy.

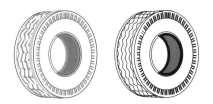

On the other hand, very slick surfaces are hard to drive on. Little or no friction allows too much movement. This is why cars can slip and slide when surfaces are wet or icy. Different types of tire treads give wheels extra traction, keeping them from slipping.

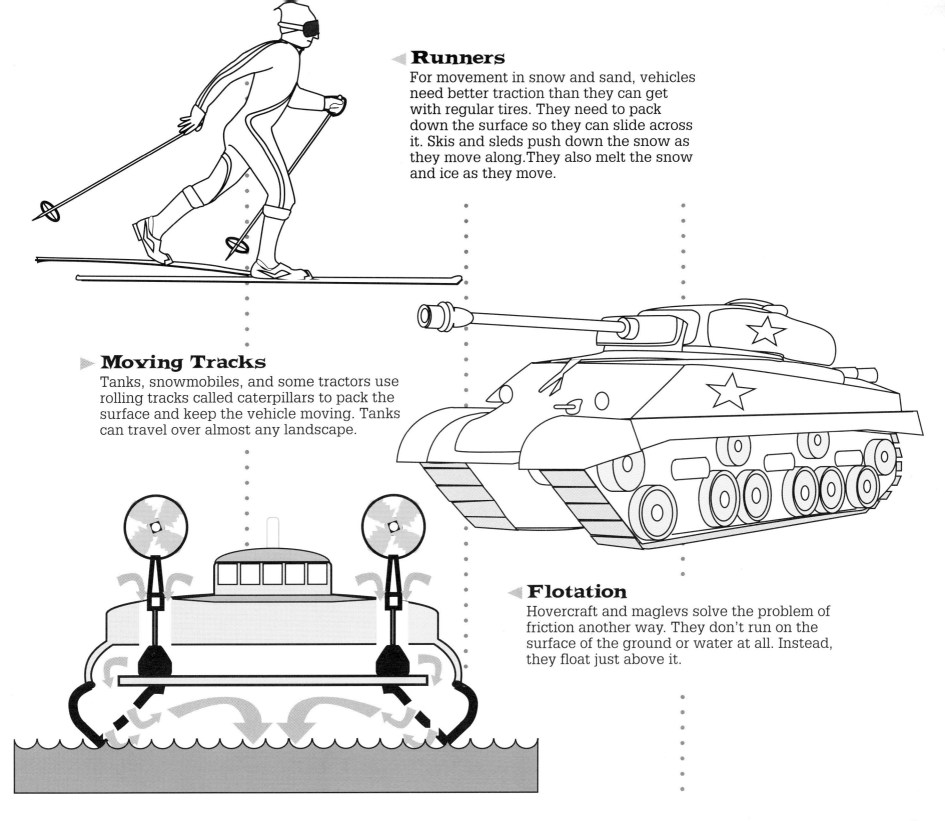

◀ Runners

For movement in snow and sand, vehicles need better traction than they can get with regular tires. They need to pack down the surface so they can slide across it. Skis and sleds push down the snow as they move along. They also melt the snow and ice as they move.

▶ Moving Tracks

Tanks, snowmobiles, and some tractors use rolling tracks called caterpillars to pack the surface and keep the vehicle moving. Tanks can travel over almost any landscape.

◀ Flotation

Hovercraft and maglevs solve the problem of friction another way. They don't run on the surface of the ground or water at all. Instead, they float just above it.

Land Travel ▸ Basics

Working With Air

Once you have solved traction, the next big problem in land transportation is getting rid of drag. Drag occurs when air hits anything that moves. Drag causes vehicles to use up more energy. It slows them down, just like friction does.

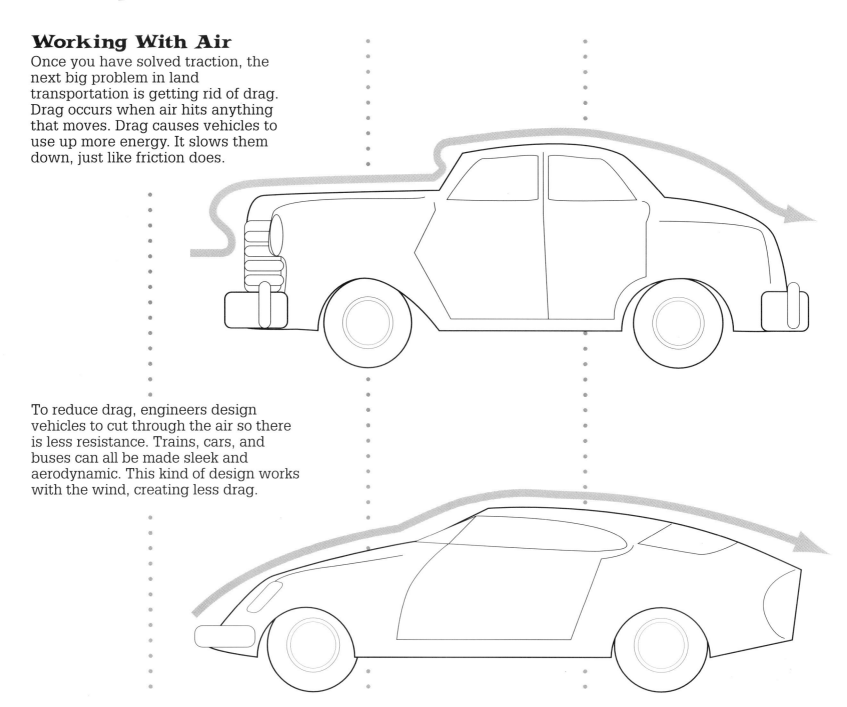

To reduce drag, engineers design vehicles to cut through the air so there is less resistance. Trains, cars, and buses can all be made sleek and aerodynamic. This kind of design works with the wind, creating less drag.

▶ Defying Gravity

Gravity is a natural force. We see it in action when something falls to Earth like a ball thrown in the air. We feel gravity as weight. The more something weighs, the more the Earth pulls it down. And the more the Earth pulls down on something, the more energy is needed to move it.

◀ As much as possible, vehicles need to be lightweight. But they also need to be strong. Making a vehicle out of cotton candy would probably not be a good idea.

▶ Today scientists are creating more materials that are tough but don't weigh a lot. These materials are chemical mixtures called composites. They're lightweight and strong, and most can be recycled.

89

Land Travel ▶ In the Future

IN THE 21ST CENTURY, people will have more ways to move from place to place. Here are some possible changes to look for:

Fast and efficient **High Speed Trains** will replace some air travel for passage between major cities.

Light Rails, including **Maglevs,** will take passengers to points outside the city limits and connect cities close to one another.

City Trains, including **Subways, Monorails,** and **Elevated Lines,** will expand in many cities. Improved computer braking systems will allow these trains to travel faster. Many will be programmed to run without a crew.

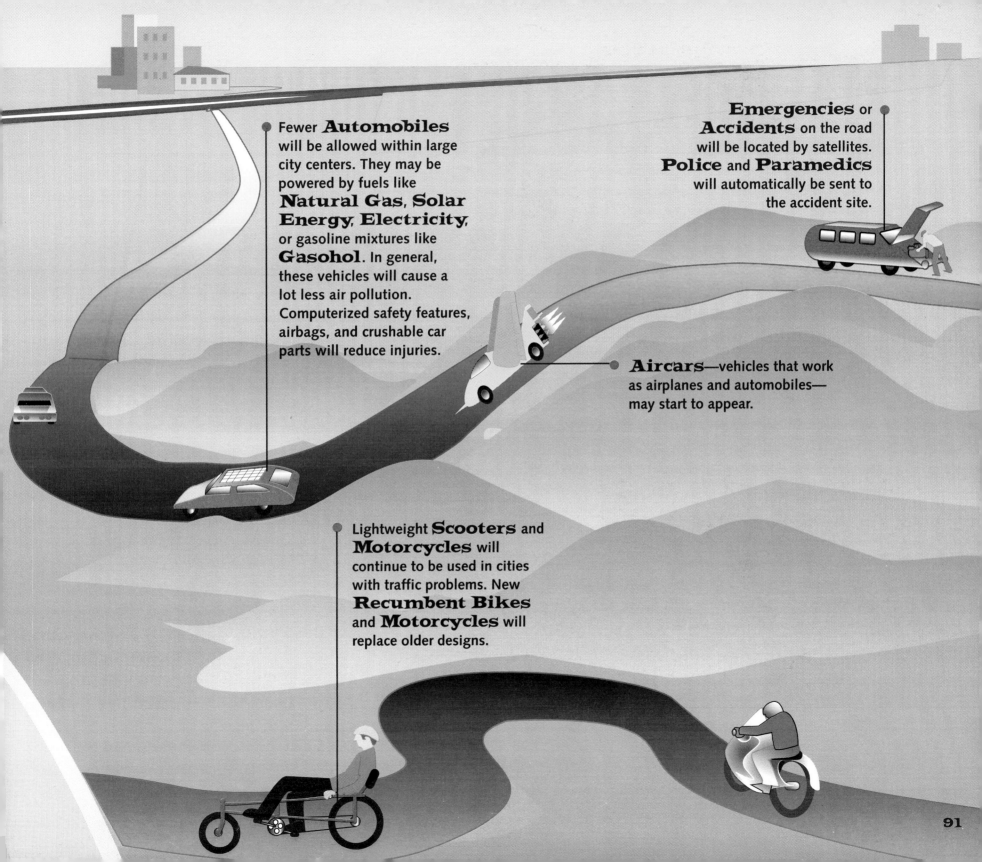

Fewer **Automobiles** will be allowed within large city centers. They may be powered by fuels like **Natural Gas, Solar Energy, Electricity,** or gasoline mixtures like **Gasohol**. In general, these vehicles will cause a lot less air pollution. Computerized safety features, airbags, and crushable car parts will reduce injuries.

Emergencies or **Accidents** on the road will be located by satellites. **Police** and **Paramedics** will automatically be sent to the accident site.

Aircars—vehicles that work as airplanes and automobiles—may start to appear.

Lightweight **Scooters** and **Motorcycles** will continue to be used in cities with traffic problems. New **Recumbent Bikes** and **Motorcycles** will replace older designs.

Manned Maneuvering Units (MMUs)

WHEN ASTRONAUTS first began to walk in space, they were tethered, or tied, to the spacecraft. Fastened in this way, they could move outside the craft and work in space without worrying about floating away. But sometimes the tether got in the way while they were doing their jobs. And it didn't really provide a way for astronauts to steer themselves as they walked or flew in space.

The Manned Maneuvering Unit (MMU) was designed to change that. The unit uses small jets to help the astronaut move around in the same way that an aircraft would. The unit attaches to the astronaut's space suit. It holds two tanks of nitrogen and can be refilled in space.

The MMU has eight thrusters. Each of the thrusters has three jet nozzles that point in different directions. The twenty-four jets shoot out nitrogen gas. The jets work like tiny rocket engines. Using them, astronauts can move in whichever direction they choose.

▲ Space Walking
Astronaut Bruce McCandless uses his manned-maneuvering unit to take a spin above the planet.

Fuel Tank

Nitrogen Jets

▲ Lunar Landing

This view from space was hard for some to believe. Human beings had made their first extraterrestrial (outside Earth's atmosphere) landing.

TRANSPORTATION FIRST: *Moon Walk*

In 1961, President John Kennedy made a promise that the United States would send a man to the moon and return him safely by the end of the decade. Americans found it a little hard to believe. The Soviet Union had had some success in their space missions. But the U.S. hadn't even gotten a person into orbit. The moon was over 200,000 miles away!

Still, the President had spoken and the National Aeronautics and Space Administration (NASA) set to work figuring out how to get a man to the moon. Its plan had three stages. First, get a spacecraft into orbit around the Earth. Then, break out of that orbit and fly to the moon and go into orbit there. Next, land a separate vehicle on the moon itself, a vehicle that could return to the orbiting spacecraft.

The early flights of the Apollo program were designed to test the different stages of the moon mission. Finally, in July 1969, just months away from Kennedy's deadline, Apollo 11 was ready to go. In an earlier Apollo flight, astronauts had gone into orbit around the moon. This time, though, human beings would actually land there, get out, and look around.

Buzz Aldrin, Michael Collins, and Neil Armstrong were the astronauts selected for the mission. Collins would operate the main spacecraft while Aldrin and Armstrong would use the lunar module to set down on the moon. The flight went off as planned.

Three days later on July 19, the astronauts reached the moon's orbit. The next day, Aldrin and Armstrong got into the lunar module. Coming down on the surface of the moon, Aldrin noticed they were about to land in a field of boulders. With only a few seconds of fuel left, Armstrong took control and piloted the lander safely down onto a smoother surface. He named the spot Tranquility Base. Once on the ground, the astronauts gradually got used to the moon's low gravity. They discovered bouncing worked better than trying to walk.

A few days later, people on Earth were treated to an unusual snapshot. The astronauts had taken a photo of the blue Earth rising over the horizon of the moon.

For more about Space Transportation **GO TO PAGE 108**

Motorcycles

MOTORCYCLES have almost all the advantages of bikes—they can move through traffic and are easy to park. Instead of leg muscles, though, motorcycles usually use a small gas engine to turn their wheels. This makes them heavier than bicycles and it also gives them a lot more power.

Like bicycles, motorcycles come in different styles, depending upon their use. Cruisers, touring, sport, and dirt bikes are the main types. Motorcycles have become more popular in recent years. In the United States alone, there are more than four million riders.

Older-style motorcycles have many of their working parts exposed. Modern cycles often have fairings, lightweight coverings that help cut down on drag or wind resistance. Fairings also help to protect engines and other parts from damage and wear.

Like bicyclists, motorcycle riders use their bodies to control their bikes. Because they are exposed while moving at high speed, cyclists have to wear heavy protective clothing and a strong helmet.

▲ Motorcycle Styles
"Biker" clothes can be colorful as well as good protection.

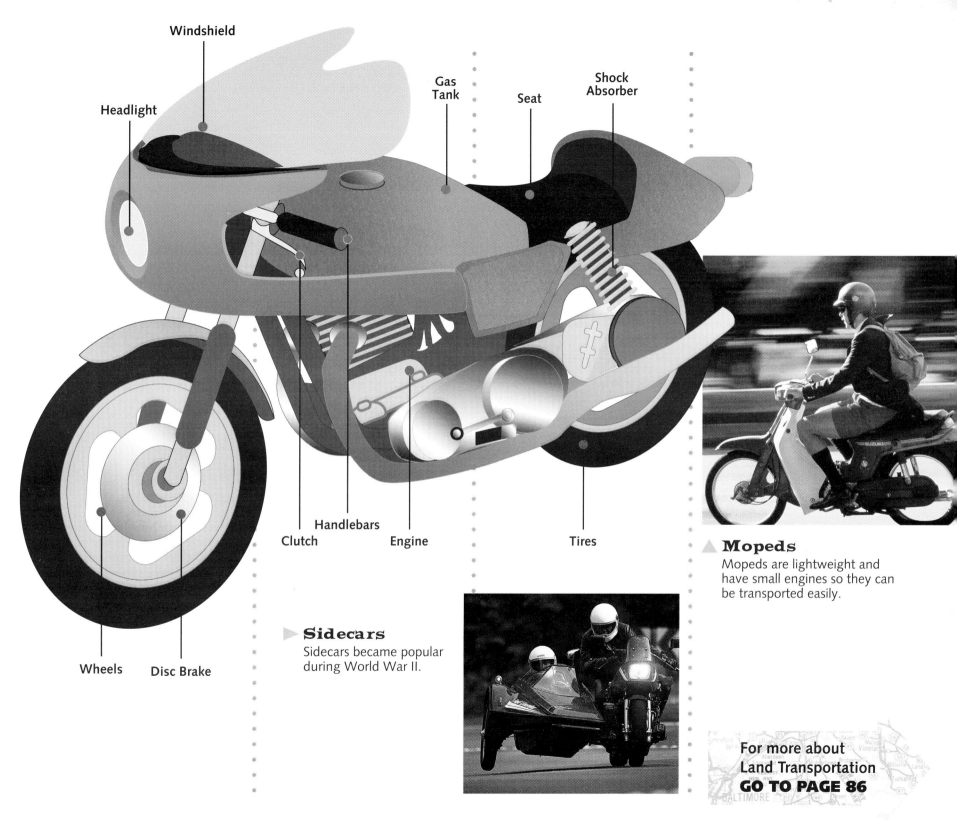

Windshield

Headlight

Gas
Tank

Seat

Shock
Absorber

Handlebars

Clutch

Engine

Tires

Wheels

Disc Brake

Mopeds

Mopeds are lightweight and have small engines so they can be transported easily.

Sidecars

Sidecars became popular during World War II.

For more about
Land Transportation
GO TO PAGE 86

Rafts

RAFTS ARE the simplest kind of water vehicle. Instead of a curved hull, rafts have a flat platform that floats on top of the water. Sometimes pontoons are attached to the platform to help keep the raft surface above water.

Thousands of people who live near the water use rafts for transportation. Many others use rafts for emergencies and for sport. Life rafts are included on ships and airplanes for safety.

The first raft designs were probably tree trunks tied together with vines. Simple rafts like these are still used in very rough water. Modern rafts replace the wood with materials like rubber, fiberglass, and acetate. Watertight compartments add safety—if one part is damaged, the others will continue to float.

Some rafts have small engines attached to them. Oars, paddles, or poles are used to move other rafts around in the water and to steer. Rafts without engines generally have no rudder and they can be steered in only a limited way. A strong current will almost always carry a raft along in its direction.

◀ Whitewater Rafters
Though they don't exactly provide a relaxing journey, whitewater rafts are a fun way to get down the Colorado River.

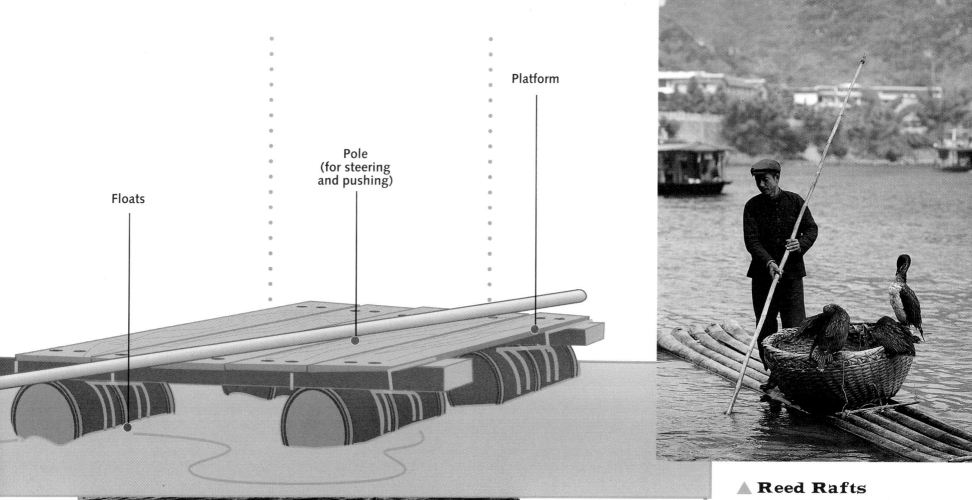

Floats

Pole
(for steering
and pushing)

Platform

▲ Reed Rafts
Many different types of
woven rafts are used by
tropical fisherman.

◀ Raft Rescue
The U.S. Coast
Guard rescues
a group of
refugees.

For more about
Water Transportation
GO TO PAGE 132

Roads and Highways

FROM A SINGLE-LANE, stone path deep in the mountains of Peru to an eight-lane superhighway in Los Angeles, roads are a big part of transportation.

Like other structures, modern roads must be designed and built. The way a road is constructed can change depending upon the materials and labor available. In China, where people are plentiful and machines are scarce, a single roadway is sometimes built by hundreds of thousands of people. In California, on the other hand, the Los Angeles superhighways were built using fewer people—but many machines. Large rollers and rock-crushers prepared the surface while other machines poured out miles of asphalt in just minutes.

Almost all roads are layered on top of a very firm surface. The layers may include gravel, stone, or clay. Most large roads have concrete or asphalt as the top layer. Crushed, smoothed glass pieces or other shiny materials are sometimes mixed into the top layer to help drivers see better at night.

Most roads, no matter how they are made, are designed before they are built. Planners figure out where the road should go, and what kind of materials need to be used in building it. Engineers must decide where tunnels, curves, and bridges need to be placed and how much traffic the road must serve.

Road Manners
Cars in several countries—including Japan and Great Britain—are designed with the steering column on the right. The rest of the world drives on the left.

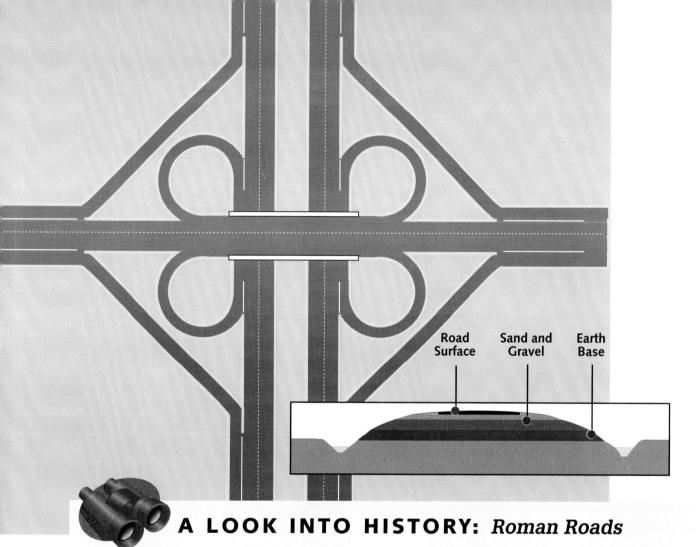

Road Surface	Sand and Gravel	Earth Base

▲ Highways for the Environment

Highway I-70 in Colorado travels through a canyon along the Colorado River. Designers had to figure out ways to build the road without hurting the natural environment. Here they are working on a piece of roadway that is built on columns on the edge of the canyon.

A LOOK INTO HISTORY: *Roman Roads*

Roads were being built more than 2,500 years ago by the Chinese and the Persians. The Incas of Peru carved out 10,000 miles of roadways along the cliffs of the Andes Mountains.

The ancient Romans, though, were probably the greatest of all road builders. In putting together their vast empire, the Romans built over 50,000 miles of roads—from East Africa to Britain. Sections of these roads still exist.

The Romans were legendary for creating roads that were straight as an arrow. This often meant breaking through earth and stone barriers. Because they had no real explosives (dynamite hadn't been invented), Roman laborers and soldiers would heat the rocks and then throw cold water on them. The sudden change in temperature would cause the stone to break apart.

Romans were the first to figure out that roads lasted longer if they were a little higher than the ground they ran through. They piled up dirt on the roadway before covering it with large stones, creating the first "highways." These roadways were up to 30 feet wide and could serve traffic moving in both directions. The Romans also discovered how to make concrete, but the recipe was lost for over a thousand years after Rome fell.

Perhaps the most famous of the Roman roads was the Via Appia, or the Appian Way. This single highway stretched 132 miles, connecting Rome to Southern Italy.

For more about Land Transportation GO TO PAGE 86

Skis

SKIS are runners that are attached to the feet with straps. The skier moves by gliding along on snow. Hand-held poles help the skier push off and stay balanced.

Though skis are used mostly for recreation, in snowbound areas cross-country skiing is also a form of transportation. For this type of travel, lighter skis are used and skiers do a combination of walking and gliding. Advanced skiers can actually do a kind of running on skis.

The first skis, made of wood, were designed in Norway in the mid-1800s. Modern skis use lightweight materials, usually plastic combined with metal or fiberglass. A narrow groove is carved along the base of the ski to help keep it moving straight. Steel edges help control the ski, cutting into the snow or ice as the skier glides. They also protect the rest of the ski from wear.

Snow Rescue
Sometimes the only way to reach lost or injured people in snowbound areas is on skis.

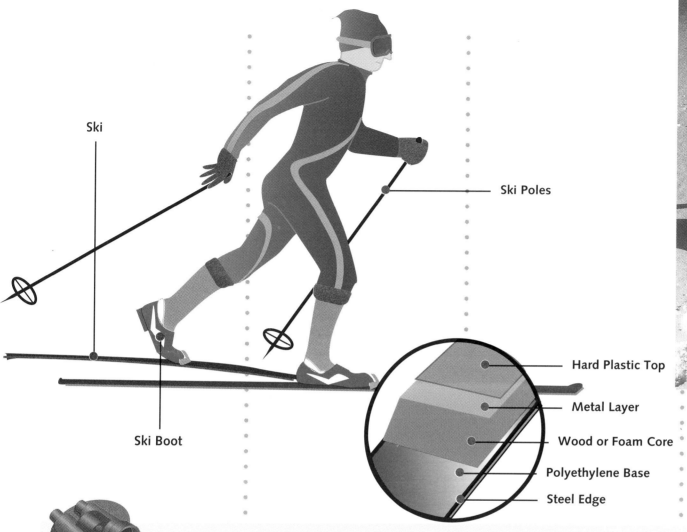

Ski

Ski Poles

Ski Boot

Hard Plastic Top

Metal Layer

Wood or Foam Core

Polyethylene Base

Steel Edge

▲ Snowshoes

Snowshoes, like skis, are used to travel through snow. An Arctic people, the Denes, invented the snowshoe centuries ago.

A LOOK INTO HISTORY: *Finnish Skiers in World War II*

The people of Finland have always been known for their impressive skiing. And their courage. During World War II, the two came together.

In 1940, the Soviet Army invaded neighboring Finland. The Russians were expecting an easy victory. They had almost one million soldiers and the Finns had only 300,000.

Finnish troops, though, were prepared for the fierce cold. They were excellent skiers, familiar with their home ground. And they were fierce fighters.

The Finns dressed warmly in white uniforms that were invisible to the enemy. Speeding on their skis in the snow,

Finn soldiers would appear "out of nowhere" and take the Soviets by surprise. Then they would disappear again into the snow-covered forest.

Without any help, the Finns held off the Soviets throughout the winter of 1940. The Soviet Union eventually used heavy air power to force Finland to surrender. But Finland regained its independence following World War II.

For more about Land Transportation GO TO PAGE 86

Sleds

SLEDS are a very old form of transportation. Thousands of years ago, people put logs together and formed sledges, or sleds, to slide across the snow. Eventually animals were used to pull these sleds. Inuits and other Arctic peoples formed their sleds with animal bones and skin.

Before automobiles were common, people attached, or "clipped," clipper sleds to their carts and wagons in the winter. Sled runners moved more easily in the snow than wheels. These clipper sleds were eventually lashed together to form bobsleds.

Modern sleds are basically a sitting ski. Side-by-side metal runners support a chair or frame where passengers can ride. Dog teams are usually used to drive sleds, although in some places they are driven by horses or reindeer. Often snowmobiles are used instead of animal power.

The most common Alaskan sled is the Nome sled, or sledge. It has sides that look like a basket and can carry 1,000 pounds. In the northern part of Russia, sleds called *troikas* are drawn by a variety of animals.

Sleds
In Arctic regions, where ground transportation is limited, sleds still serve as vehicles. Inuit sleds were once made from available materials like moss, caribou bones, and seal skin.

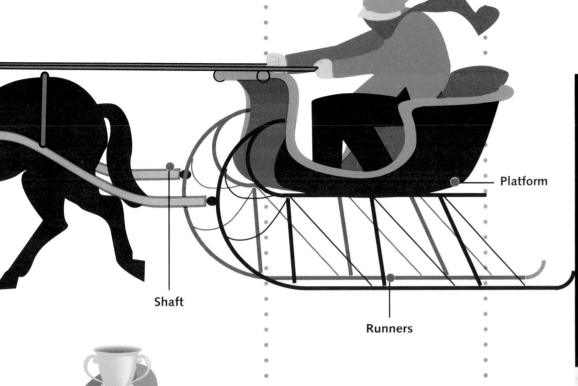

Shaft

Platform

Runners

▼ Bobsled

Bobsleds are often used for sport-riding. A bobsled is formed by two sleds called clippers joined together.

TRANSPORTATION FIRST: *Journey to the North Pole*

From the 16th century on, explorers looked for ways to reach the North Pole. In the 1700s, the Russian Vitus Bering piloted boats above the Arctic Circle and proved that Asia and America were separated by water, but that was as far as he got.

In the 1800s, explorers began to search for the Northwest Passage, an Arctic ocean route that would connect the Atlantic and Pacific oceans. Team after team of explorers set out to find the route, only to meet disaster. Boats were crushed in seas swollen with ice. One team tried to fly a balloon over the Pole only to crash and freeze to death in the snow. Another group of explorers simply disappeared.

Robert Peary saw the failures of these teams and decided that some other way had to be found to reach the Pole. Like many others, he used a boat to get up above the Arctic Circle.

But once there he abandoned the water route and continued with sleds pulled by dog teams. Groups of Eskimos went with Peary and his companion Matthew Henson. The Eskimos served as guides. Using specially built, wide sleds the Eskimos carted supplies and set up camp ahead of Peary.

When he was within striking distance of the Pole, Peary set off on sleds with a small party including Henson and four Eskimos—Coqueeh, Ootah, Eginwah, and Seegloo. On April 6, 1909, the group reached the Pole and built an igloo. Several explorers disputed Peary's claim. But recent studies have shown that he actually was the first to reach the Pole.

For more about Land Transportation GO TO PAGE 86

Snowmobiles

SNOWMOBILES were known at first as "motor sleds." Most still have two short skis, or runners, at the front. A small gasoline engine turns a wide track, or belt at the back. This action moves the machine through the snow, as the driver steers with the handlebars.

Snowmobiles have replaced sleds in Arctic and subarctic areas. Or they may be used instead of animals to pull sleds. A Canadian, Joseph-Armand Bombardier, developed the first small snowmobile in the early 1950's. Snowmobiles can carry one or two people and can be used for delivery, recreation, and rescues in snowy places.

Like motorcycles and cars, snowmobiles use gasoline engines and they are noisy. Many people complain that these vehicles can hurt the unspoiled environments in which they are often used. Snowmobile manufacturers have improved designs over the years to make the vehicles quieter.

Sport Snowmobiles

Snowmobile clubs often form networks of trails in northern areas. Most snowmobiles can reach speeds of 50 miles per hour. Some racers have doubled that rate.

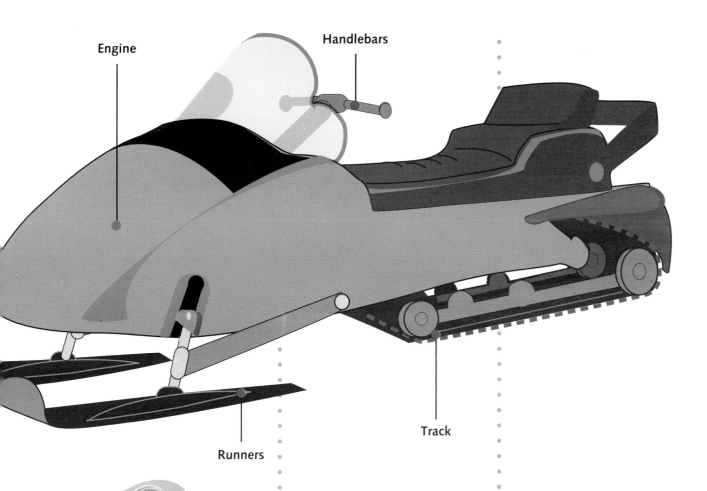

Engine

Handlebars

Track

Runners

▲ **Snow Tractor**
Caterpillar tractors use rolling tracks to move through snow or rough terrain.

SCIENCE CLOSE-UP: *How Tracks Work*

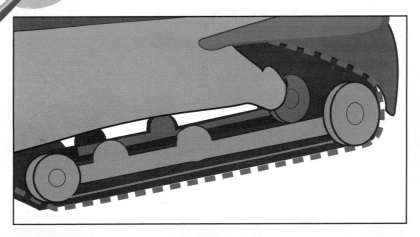

If you have a rough surface to travel over, you can clear it. Or you can take your own smooth surface with you as you travel. This is how tracks work. Snowmobiles, tanks, and some tractors all use rubber or steel moving tracks. The tread of the tracks is rolled around an endless belt that the wheels of the vehicle ride on.

Tracks allow vehicles to ride on rocky or soft ground or snow without a problem. But they can be hard on the land they roll over and have to be used carefully in fragile environments.

For more about
Land Transportation
GO TO PAGE 86

Space Shuttle

THE Space Shuttle is a reusable vehicle that works in two ways. During take-off and while in orbit, the shuttle functions as a spacecraft. But when it lands, it works like a glider.

The shuttle is carried into space by five big rocket engines. Other smaller engines move the craft around once it's in orbit. While the shuttle is in orbit, it is used as both a vehicle and a laboratory. With it, astronauts have launched satellites, repaired space equipment, and conducted many experiments.

During the next decade, the National Aeronautics and Space Administration (NASA) mission specialists will use the shuttle for a variety of tasks. They will map the surface of the earth using radar, or radio waves, and begin building the space station.

Because the shuttle reenters the atmosphere at very high speeds (Mach 25), it gets very hot when it returns to Earth. The skin of the shuttle is covered with special glass or ceramic tiles that won't melt. These tiles also protect the crew in the cabin from the intense heat. When the shuttle glides in for its landing, a parachute helps it come to a stop.

▲ **Shuttle in Space**
The cargo bay doors of the shuttle open to reveal a space laboratory where onboard scientists can carry out a variety of experiments.

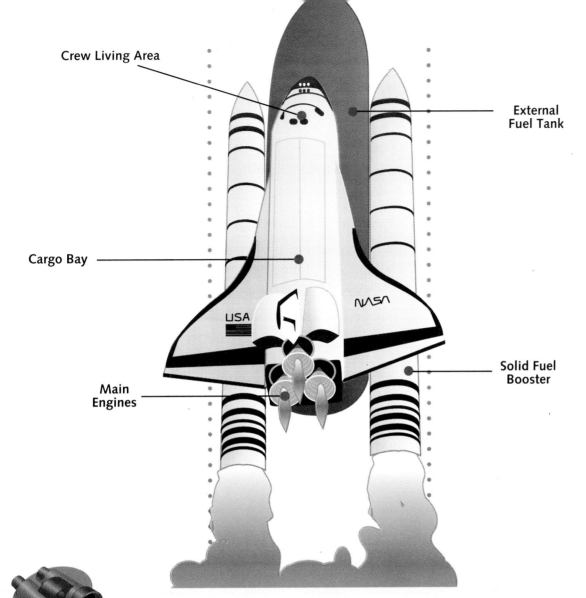

Crew Living Area

External Fuel Tank

Cargo Bay

Solid Fuel Booster

Main Engines

▲ **Working in Space**
Astronauts are trained to do a variety of jobs in space. One of the tools they can use is the CanadArm a robotic arm with shoulder, elbow, and wrist joints.

A LOOK INTO HISTORY: *Rocket Science*

The idea of a rocket is fairly simple and very old. A basic rocket is made by putting fuel into a tube closed at one end and burning it. Expanding gases from the burning fuel go out the open end of the rocket, making it go forward. Most fireworks work this way.

As for exactly how old rockets are, no one is sure. But a type of rocket is mentioned in a Chinese manuscript that was written 1,000 years ago. Modern rockets that take people into space are more complicated. Their design owes a lot to the work of Robert Goddard, a scientist who worked in the 1920s and 30s. He was the person who first figured out how to make rockets that could travel in space. Solid fuels, like gunpowder, aren't efficient enough to lift heavy loads into space. And they can't be stopped or started easily. Goddard figured out how to use more controllable liquid fuels to power his rocket.

For more about
Space Transportation
GO TO PAGE 108

Space Travel ▸ Basics

Getting Into Space

In order to get into space and stay there, spacecraft need a lot of speed. That means they need a lot of power. They get both from rocket engines. These engines use both fuel and liquid oxygen. Inside the engine the two are mixed together and ignited.

1

◀ Hot gases blast out of the engine, pushing the rocket forward at supersonic speed.

2

▶ **Shuttle Craft**
Rockets help propel spacecraft outside the Earth's atmosphere. The Space Shuttle flies into space attached to rocket boosters. These boosters add their power to the shuttle's own engines so the spacecraft can go fast and far enough into space to orbit the Earth.

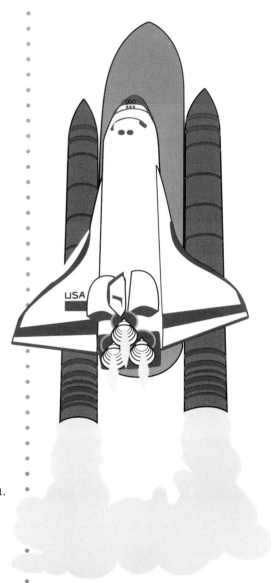

▶ Orbiting

3 Once the craft is in space, smaller rocket engines move it into orbit, a natural path around the planet. Spacecraft do not have to use their engines when they are in orbit except to change their position or orbit path.

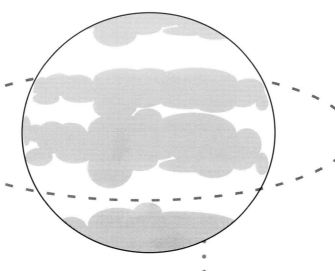

4

▶ Changes in Space

When the craft completes its orbits, rocket engines are used to slow it down. Gravity causes it to fall swiftly through the atmosphere—back to Earth.

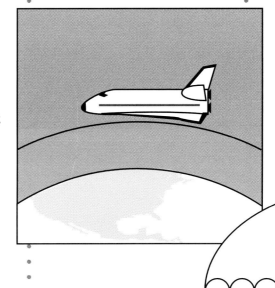

5

▶ Returning to Earth

When the first space flights returned to Earth, the capsules—the part of the rocket containing the astronauts—fell into the ocean. The astronauts and their craft were usually rescued by helicopter. Though the astronauts could return to space later, the capsules weren't reusable. Today Space Shuttles are designed to land on a runway and be reused.

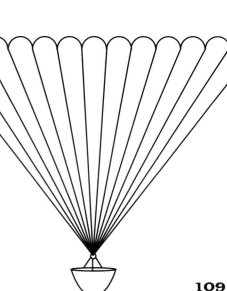

Space Travel ▸ In the Future

IN THE 21ST CENTURY, space will be occupied by hundreds of satellites and one or more space stations. Vehicles will travel to and from the space station from Earth and other planets.

The **Spaceplane** will eventually replace the Space Shuttle. It will take off like a regular airliner, then accelerate to very high speeds. It will then travel through space, landing like a regular plane. The plane will be used in space, but also for long-distance transportation on Earth.

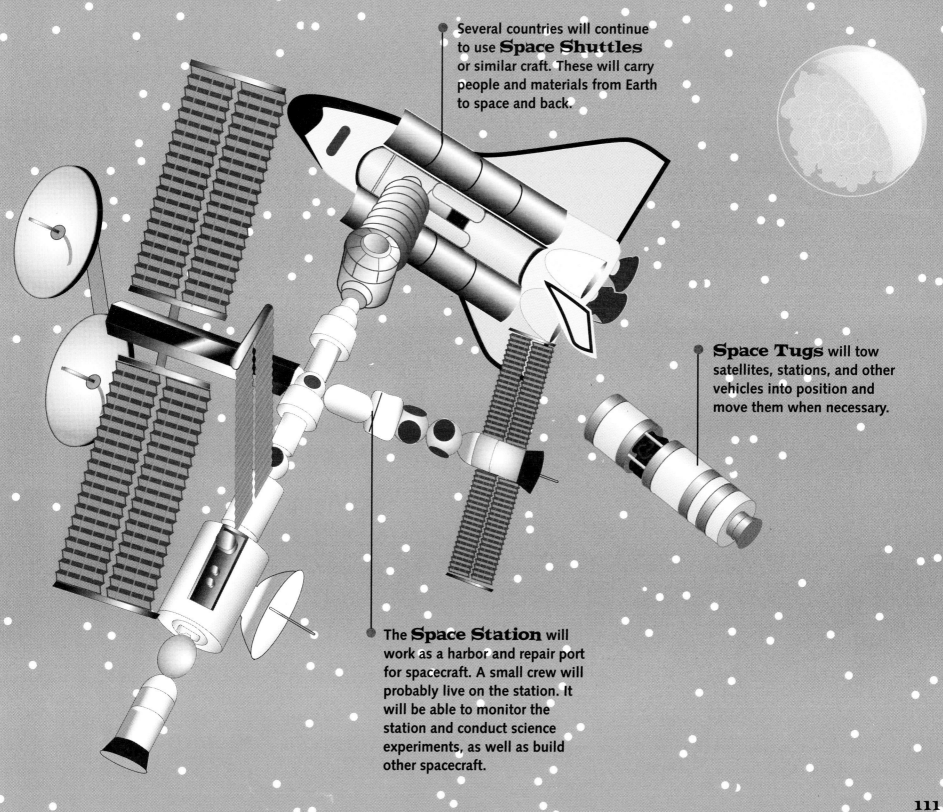

Several countries will continue to use **Space Shuttles** or similar craft. These will carry people and materials from Earth to space and back.

Space Tugs will tow satellites, stations, and other vehicles into position and move them when necessary.

The **Space Station** will work as a harbor and repair port for spacecraft. A small crew will probably live on the station. It will be able to monitor the station and conduct science experiments, as well as build other spacecraft.

Submarines

SUBMARINES are watercraft that work—and look—a lot like airships. Instead of an envelope filled with gas, subs have ballast tanks that can be filled with air or water. Air in the tanks lightens the submarine and lets it float. When the tanks are filled with water, the submarine gets heavier and sinks.

Under and above water, submarines are driven by propellers. Fins called hydroplanes help the boat to dive to the sea floor or return to the surface of the water. A rudder is used for steering. Subs use diesel power only when they are above the water. Diesel engines need air to work so subs switch to electric power when they submerge. Modern military craft often use nuclear fuel to provide their power. Nuclear submarines can travel tens of thousands of miles without refueling.

Submarines are used almost entirely for defense and warfare. Submarine weapons usually include missiles and torpedoes, sometimes with nuclear warheads.

◀ **Nuclear First**

United States Ohio Class Submarines are nuclear-powered. They carry two dozen *Trident* missiles.

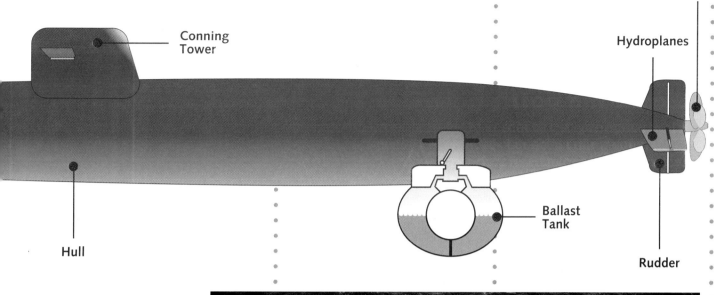

Conning
Tower

Propeller

Hydroplanes

Hull

Ballast
Tank

Rudder

▼ Inside the Submarine
A modern nuclear sub carries a crew of over 100 in comfort. Because there are no windows it's impossible to tell whether it is night or day outside the sub. Lights are dimmed during "night" hours to mimic natural light.

▶ Nuclear First
U.S.S. Nautilus, the Navy's first atomic-powered submarine, on its first sea trials.

A LOOK INTO HISTORY: *The* Nautilus

In the summer of 1954, a nuclear submarine began a strange and remarkable voyage under a block of ice. The U.S.S. Nautilus traveled underneath the Arctic ice cap from one side to another in just four days.

Other subs had ducked under the ice briefly before. But a trip all the way under the Arctic cap had been impossible. For one thing, until the mid-1950s all subs used diesel fuel. That meant they had to resurface and refuel often. But the Nautilus was nuclear-powered. It could stay underwater for weeks at a time.

Still, going under the ice cap was frightening. People worried that the sub might be crushed between the ocean floor and the thick ice cap above. The Nautilus' first voyage almost proved them right. It ended in failure when the submarine was nearly trapped by deep ice. It escaped, but with only a few feet to spare.

But the Nautilus crew tried again during the summer of 1954 when the ice was warmer and thinner. This time they succeeded. Today, subs routinely travel under the Arctic ice.

For more about Water Transportation GO TO PAGE 132

Submersibles

SUBMERSIBLES work a little like elevators—and a lot like submarines. Like elevators, submersibles carry people up and down. Like submarines, they are designed to travel underwater.

Submersibles grew out of underwater tools created during World War II. Today they are used for all sorts of jobs, including charting the ocean surface and locating and retrieving sunken objects. The United States Navy and other naval forces use submersibles for submarine rescue. In some resort areas, submersibles now take tourists for undersea visits.

Like submarines, most submersibles use ballast tanks to move up and down. Because they descend much farther than submarines, they are built to withstand great water pressure.

Maximum Underwater Working Depths	
VEHICLE	**DEPTH**
Submersible Suits	500 FEET
Nuclear Submarines	2,300 FEET
Standard Submersible	11,000 FEET
Advanced Submersible	20,000 FEET
Bathyscaphe	36,000 FEET

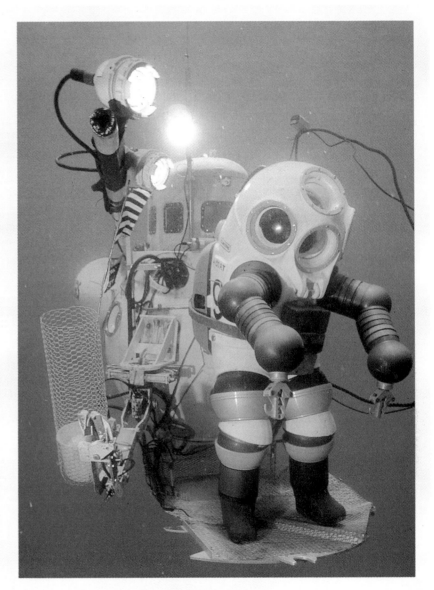

▲ **Submersible Suits**
New designs for submersibles include individual submersible suits. These water suits allow researchers to descend to up to 500 feet.

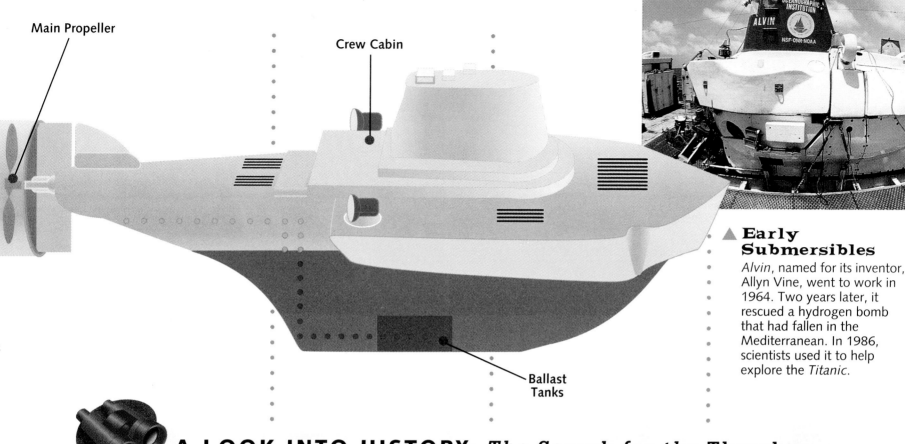

Main Propeller

Crew Cabin

Ballast Tanks

▲ **Early Submersibles**

Alvin, named for its inventor, Allyn Vine, went to work in 1964. Two years later, it rescued a hydrogen bomb that had fallen in the Mediterranean. In 1986, scientists used it to help explore the *Titanic*.

A LOOK INTO HISTORY: *The Search for the* Thresher

In April 1963, the U.S. Navy launched the greatest sea search in history. Six destroyers, two submarines, two squadrons of Navy aircraft and a pair of submarine rescue vehicles joined several other ships just off the New England coast. They were searching for a lost submarine–not just any submarine, but the Thresher.

The Thresher, SSN593, was the lead vessel in a new class of attack submarines just launched by the Navy. But within a year of its launch, the prized Thresher had disappeared with 129 men on board. The intensive search for the sub was centered around the area where it had broadcast its last radio message.

After days of searching, a possible wreck site was finally located. But it was lying on the ocean floor, too deep for any rescue vehicles to go down and take a closer look.

The Navy ordered that the bathyscaphe Trieste be sent to the scene of the wreck. This deepwater submersible vehicle had

already descended to the deepest part of the ocean floor, 36,000 feet down. Now its electronic and photographic equipment would be used to make certain that this wreck was, in fact, the Thresher.

The Trieste made a series of dives through the following months. Finally the captain of the submersible came upon what he described as "a large automobile junkyard." Using remote control he clamped the submersible's arm onto a section of twisted brass pipe. When it was brought to the surface, the pipe gave the answer everyone was looking for, but no one wanted to hear. The five-foot pipe was marked 593—the call number of the Thresher.

To this day, no one is entirely sure why the Thresher went down. But the Trieste allowed scientists to study the debris well enough to figure out why the Thresher sank. The hull was crushed when the ship descended into water that was too deep for it.

For more about **Water Transportation** **GO TO PAGE 132**

Trains

POWERED by steam, diesel fuel, or electricity, trains are used for transportation all over the world. They are often the most efficient and safest way of moving freight and people from place to place.

Trains run on single (monorail) or double rails. The distance between two rails is called the gauge. The size of the gauge determines what type of train can run on the track.

Individual cars on a train are connected by couplers. Most trains ride on some type of wheels, but magnetic trains (maglevs) ride above the ground.

Trains are used for many different kinds of transportation. They carry passengers under and above the ground in cities and towns. Longer-distance trains travel throughout the countryside, carrying passengers and freight. High-speed trains now connect major cities in several countries.

Steep Grade Rails

Special train tracks allow trains to climb steep slopes. Cog wheel trains lock the train's wheels to the track to keep it from slipping downhill as it moves along.

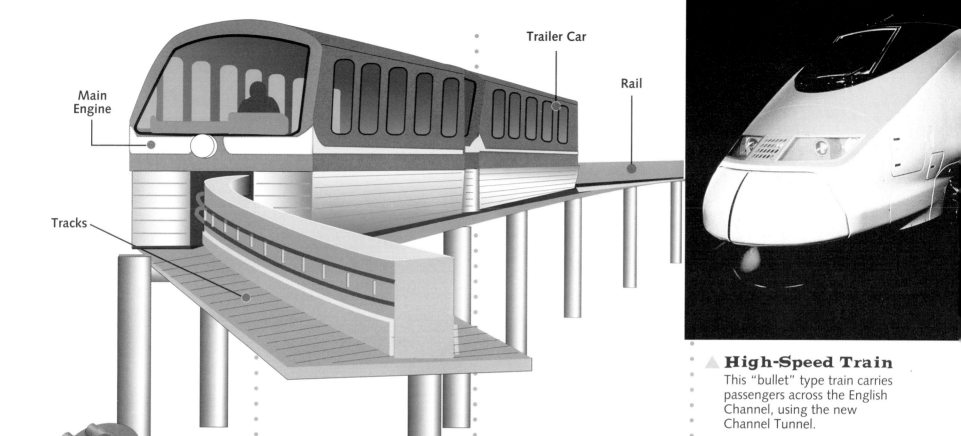

Main Engine

Trailer Car

Rail

Tracks

▲ High-Speed Train
This "bullet" type train carries passengers across the English Channel, using the new Channel Tunnel.

A LOOK INTO HISTORY: *The* Orient Express

Train rides during the 19th century were more hard work than fun. Steam-driven trains were, and still are, very hot, especially in summertime. There were no toilets or washrooms or dining cars. Stops were short and a bad-tempered train engineer might pull away as you tried to finish your dinner in the station.

The Orient Express changed all that. A young Belgian man, Georges Nagelmacker, began a new rail line through Europe in 1883. At first it ran only from Paris, France, to Berlin, Germany. But eventually the route extended all the way to

Turkey. Travel on the Express was the height of luxury. Paintings by famous artists hung in gold frames along the walls. Dinner was served on board under the soft glow of gas lamps. At night passengers slept between silk sheets with feather comforters.

As air travel became popular, the excitement of train travel passed. The last run of the Orient Express left the London station in May 1974. The publicity about this final trip made people interested in the Express once again. In the 1980s, the line was restored. Today, people can still travel on the famous Orient Express.

◀ Luxury Service
The *Orient Express* used beautiful posters to advertise its service.

For more about Land Transportation
GO TO PAGE 86

117

Trains ▶ Electric

ELECTRICITY is used more and more to power trains. Light rails like monorails and city trains are all electric. So are modern high-speed trains such as the Japanese Shinkansen, the French TGV, and the German Iceman.

Electricity is an especially good power source for trains that run in cities because it doesn't pollute the air. The electric current for trains is taken from a power plant. The electricity is usually run along a third rail, but it can sometimes be fed through an overhead line called a catenary. Electric urban trains are sometimes known as light-rails.

Many heavier trains are powered by diesel engines that make their own electricity. These trains are called diesel-electrics.

Light Rail Train
Small trains like this run between fixed points almost like a shuttle bus.

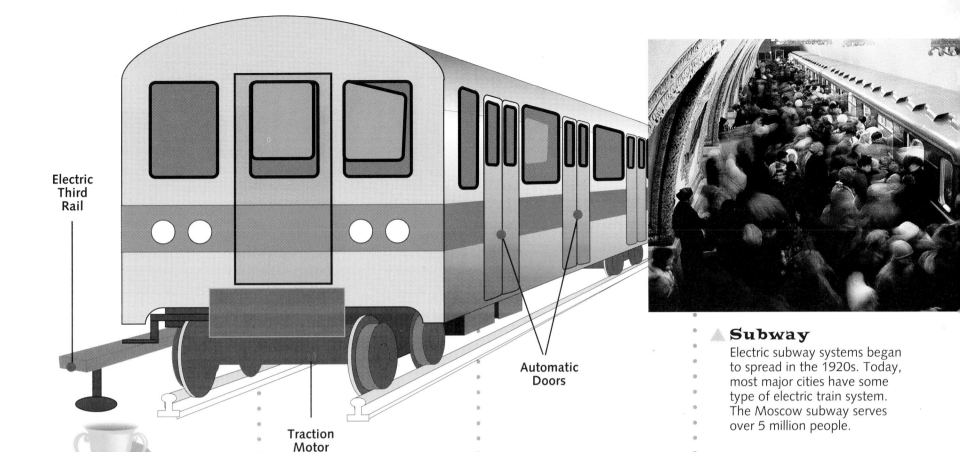

Electric Third Rail

Automatic Doors

Traction Motor

Subway

Electric subway systems began to spread in the 1920s. Today, most major cities have some type of electric train system. The Moscow subway serves over 5 million people.

TRANSPORTATION FIRST: *The London Underground*

The London Underground

The British "tube" is one of the best city train systems in the world.

In the 1800s, London was a crowded, dirty city. So many people had come to work there, the streets were nearly impossible to walk through. Roads were full of carriage traffic. What public transportation existed was unreliable and dangerous.

Finally in the 1850s, the city officials approved a plan to put a railway underneath the city. An underground railway would help people move around freely. And it wouldn't take up any valuable space aboveground.

The first subway tunnel was built, but it had problems. The fumes from the steam locomotives were fierce. Employees passed out and had to be carried out of tunnels. Passengers didn't like the unhealthy air either, even though train officials told them the fumes were good for them. Eventually large fans were put into the tunnels to blow the dirty air out.

In 1889, the London Underground was changed over to electricity. The tunnels were now cleaner and safer.

For more about
Land Transportation
GO TO PAGE 86

Trains ▸ High-Speed

WITH the arrival of jet passenger planes, many people stopped using trains for long-distance travel. Even fast trains could only move at just over 100 miles per hour. Jet airplanes easily tripled that speed.

However, in the 1960s, Japanese engineers began working on a new design for a fast train, the bullet train. This design brought train technology up-to-date and made them more competitive with airplanes. Since then several other countries have come up with designs for high-speed trains. These vehicles have reached speeds of over 300 miles per hour.

Most "bullet," or high-speed trains use simple technology to speed them along. Instead of curving tracks that cross or switch, high-speed trains use very straight tracks. This allows the train to move faster. The cars of bullet trains are sleek with curved fronts and sides. This reduces drag, or wind resistance that slows trains down.

A very different type of high-speed train is called a maglev. Maglevs use a set of magnets to lift or levitate the train above the ground. Though they run between rails, the cars are really floating. This cuts down nearly all of the friction on the train and lets it move very fast.

Because they move so fast, high-speed trains often have special disc brakes like the ones used on jet airplanes.

French High-Speed Train
A "skirt" in the design of the TGV— Train à Grand Vitesse (High-Speed Train)— keeps the French train from actually "taking off" or rising off the rails.

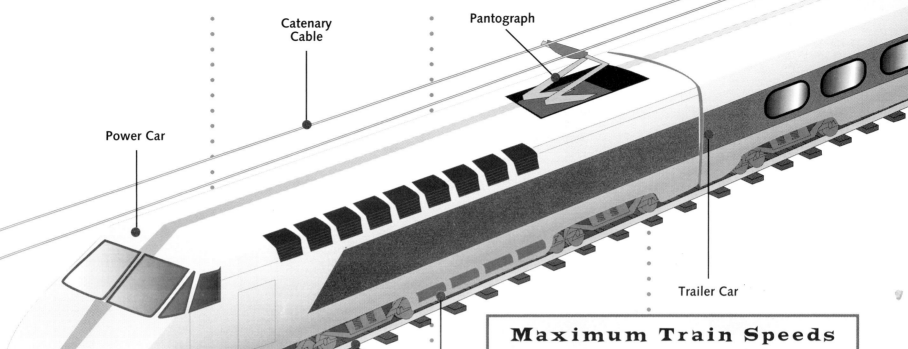

Catenary Cable

Pantograph

Power Car

Trailer Car

Side Skirt

Straight Tracks

Maximum Train Speeds

VEHICLE	YEAR	MILES PER HOUR
Steam Train	1930	125
Diesel Train	1950	130
Bullet Train (Japan)	1967	225
Ice Train (German)	1988	250
TGV Train (France)	1990	320

◄ **Maglevs**

New magnetic levitation trains called maglevs are being tested in several countries including the United States, Britain, Germany, and Japan. These trains use magnets to lift them above the ground. Super-maglevs may eventually travel thousands of miles per hour.

For more about **Land Transportation** **GO TO PAGE 86**

Trains ▶ Steam

TODAY most trains use diesel fuel or electricity for power. But steam trains still run in parts of Asia and Africa. Trains that run on steam have a simple, strong design that keeps them working for a long time. Fuels such as wood or coal are burned to heat water. The steam from the boiling water is used to move pistons that turn the wheels of the train.

Because they burn fuels such as coal to heat the water, steam trains are dirty and they pollute the air. That's why they are no longer used for transportation in cities. But in some rural areas, they are still the only means of cheap, long-distance transportation.

Steam Passenger Trains

Steam trains still provide necessary transportation in areas where other vehicles, roads, or waterways are scarce. Here a steam engine is used to push rail cars instead of pulling them.

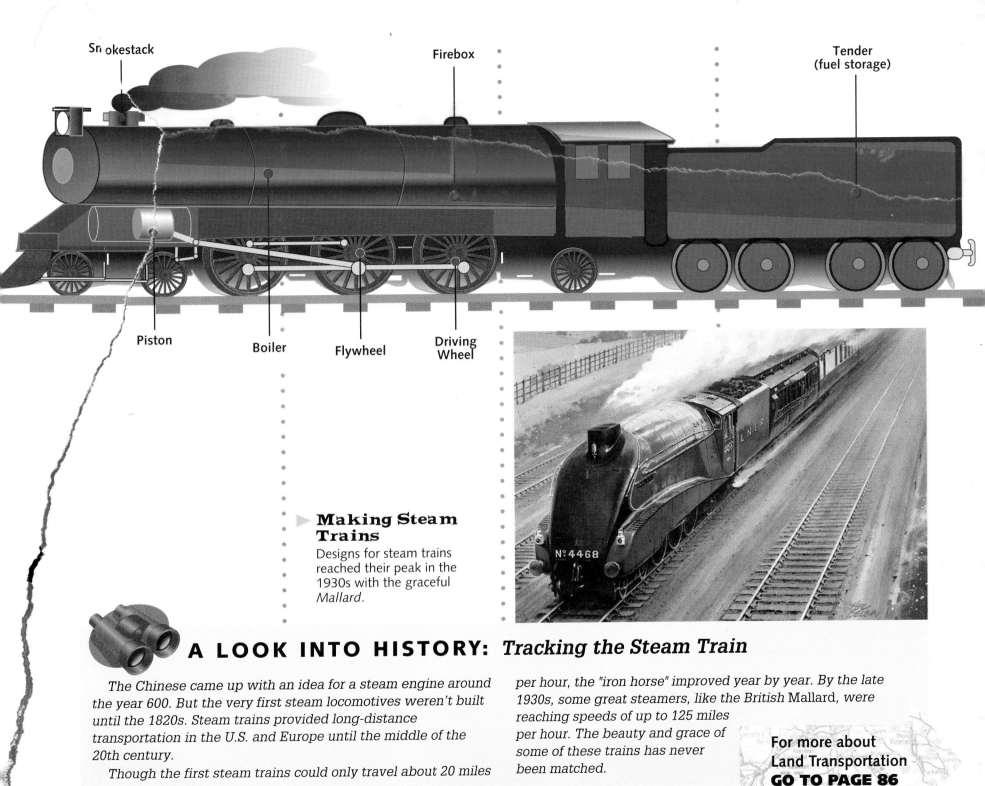

Smokestack

Firebox

Tender
(fuel storage)

Piston

Boiler

Flywheel

Driving
Wheel

Nº 4468

▶ **Making Steam Trains**

Designs for steam trains reached their peak in the 1930s with the graceful *Mallard*.

A LOOK INTO HISTORY: *Tracking the Steam Train*

The Chinese came up with an idea for a steam engine around the year 600. But the very first steam locomotives weren't built until the 1820s. Steam trains provided long-distance transportation in the U.S. and Europe until the middle of the 20th century.

Though the first steam trains could only travel about 20 miles per hour, the "iron horse" improved year by year. By the late 1930s, some great steamers, like the British *Mallard*, were reaching speeds of up to 125 miles per hour. The beauty and grace of some of these trains has never been matched.

For more about
Land Transportation
GO TO PAGE 86

Trains ► Working

TRAINS do more than carry passengers. They also move food, fuel, and other goods to places around the world. Many different types of train cars are used for freight.

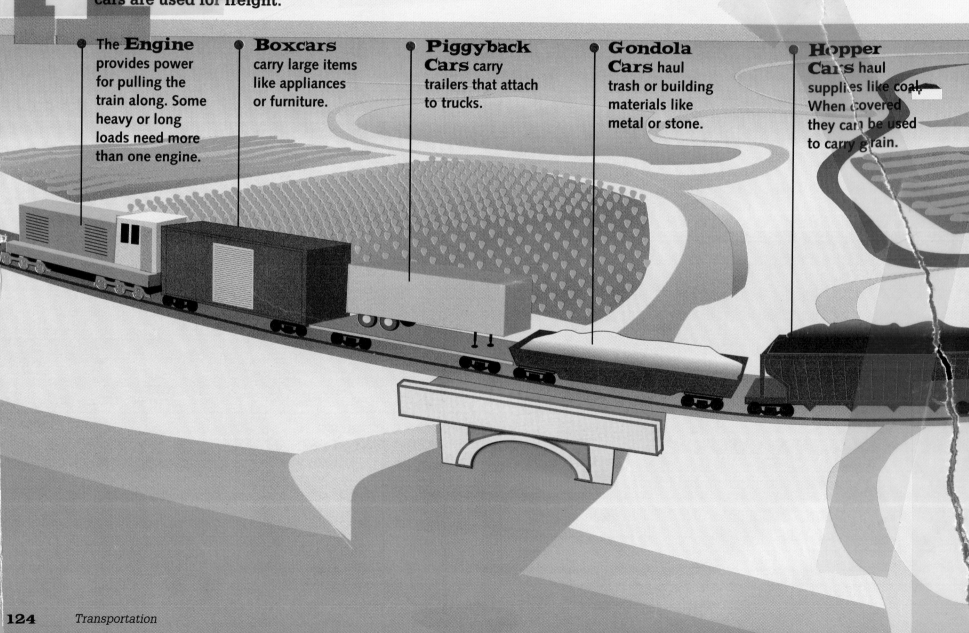

The **Engine** provides power for pulling the train along. Some heavy or long loads need more than one engine.

Boxcars carry large items like appliances or furniture.

Piggyback Cars carry trailers that attach to trucks.

Gondola Cars haul trash or building materials like metal or stone.

Hopper Cars haul supplies like coal. When covered they can be used to carry grain.

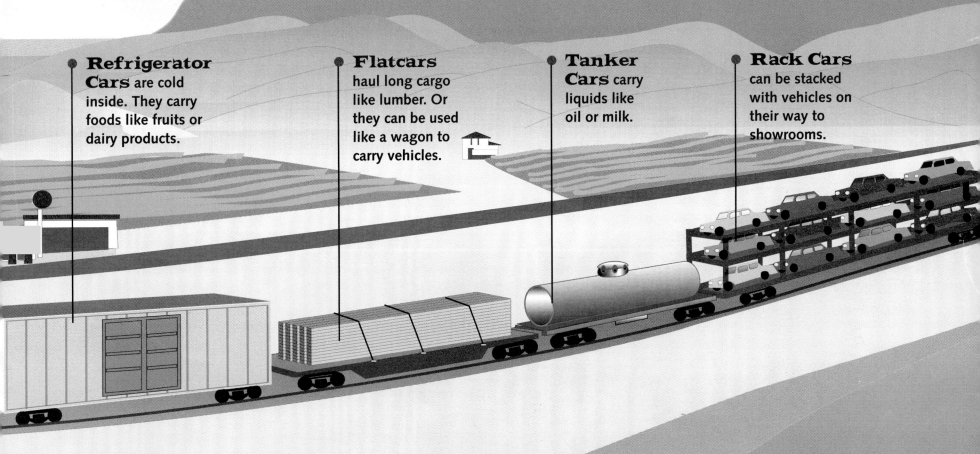

Refrigerator Cars are cold inside. They carry foods like fruits or dairy products.

Flatcars haul long cargo like lumber. Or they can be used like a wagon to carry vehicles.

Tanker Cars carry liquids like oil or milk.

Rack Cars can be stacked with vehicles on their way to showrooms.

125

Trucks

TRUCKS are built very much like automobiles. But they are designed to carry more weight, so the engine and other parts are bigger and tougher. Tires are wider with deep treads for better traction. A truck's frame is very strong and built to carry a lot of weight. Trucks may weigh as much as twenty times what a car does.

There are two basic types of trucks—rigids and semis. Rigids have the engine, cab, and body (cargo areas) all in one piece. Semis have a separate tractor (engine and cab) that pulls their trailer (a place for cargo).

Though trucks have most of the systems that cars have, there are a few differences. Unlike most automobiles, big trucks have engines that burn diesel fuel. Diesel is a thicker fuel than gasoline. In a gasoline engine the fuel/air mixture is ignited, or set on fire, with electric sparks. In a diesel engine, the fuel/air mixture is compressed or squashed until it becomes hot enough to explode.

Truck Freight

Many goods travel across countries and continents on the back of a truck. Truckers often drive straight through, stopping only for food and some "shut-eye" in their cab.

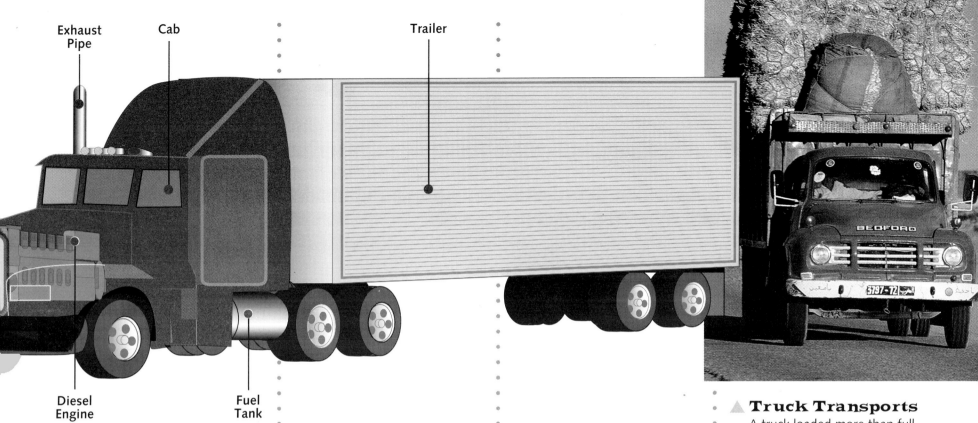

Exhaust Pipe

Cab

Trailer

Diesel Engine

Fuel Tank

▲ Truck Transports

A truck loaded more than full with hay moves down a road in Morocco.

◀ Pick-ups

People in rural areas often rely on the pick-up for hauling supplies. The tougher design of trucks helps when driving on rough roads.

For more about
Land Transportation
GO TO PAGE 86

Trucks ▸ Working

TRUCKS provide a wide range of services around the world. Many trucks are designed to perform special work. Here are some you might see on the road.

Dump Trucks have a hopper or container that flips up so they can "dump" their cargo.

Sanitation Trucks are used to collect trash. Most have rollers and packers to squash down the collected waste.

Vans are covered trucks. They can be used to move people, animals, or other cargo.

Wrecker or Tow Trucks have lifts that help to pick up broken-down cars.

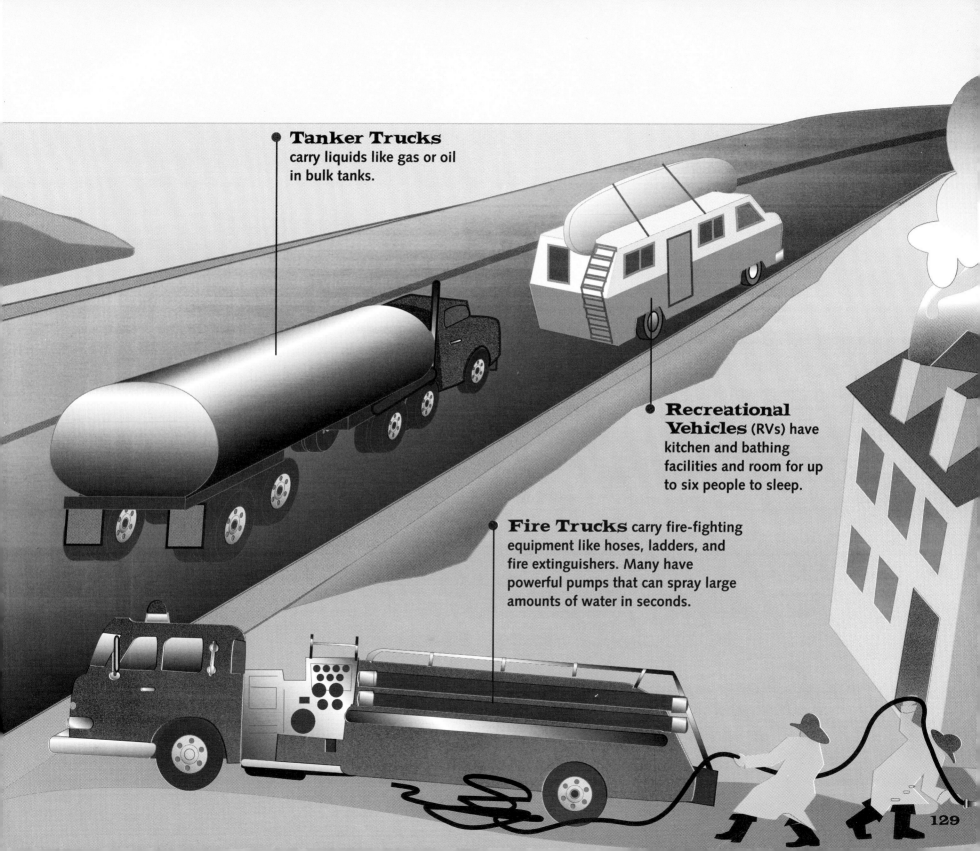

Tanker Trucks carry liquids like gas or oil in bulk tanks.

Recreational Vehicles (RVs) have kitchen and bathing facilities and room for up to six people to sleep.

Fire Trucks carry fire-fighting equipment like hoses, ladders, and fire extinguishers. Many have powerful pumps that can spray large amounts of water in seconds.

Tunnels

IMAGINE driving right through a mountain 15,000 feet high and coming out in another country. Sounds like science fiction, but thousands of people do it every day. They use the Mont Blanc tunnel on the border of France and Italy.

Like bridges, tunnels make it easier to travel across rough land and water. But they do it by making a roadway under the ground or water.

Subway tunnels carry trains underneath cities. Instead of burrowing underground, builders often use a "cut and cover" design. They cut open the ground, build the tunnel, and cover it over. Underwater tunnels are often cut into the waterbed—the earth and rock underneath the water. This makes the tunnels extra stable.

Tunnel builders use lots of high-tech equipment. Huge tunnel building machines burrow through the earth. Explosives turn solid rock to rubble. Machines shoot hundreds of tons of wet concrete to form walls.

Tunnels can be built for both road and rail vehicles. Some modern tunnels stretch for more than 30 miles. These longer tunnels have an extra service tube that is used mostly by workers. In an emergency it allows people to escape from the main tunnel.

Interstate Tunnel
Building a tunnel is one of the most difficult jobs in road construction. This one, on Interstate 70 in Colorado, cuts through a section of Glenwood Canyon.

Eurotunnel

The new tunnel under the 23-mile-wide English Channel carries rail traffic between Britain and France. Cars, buses, and trucks—as well as people—are hauled on the rail cars. The trip lasts about 35 minutes.

Digging Tunnels

One of the big problems with tunnel building is where to put all that dirt. Today's TBMs (Tunnel Building Machines), "swallow up" the dirt as they carve out the tunnel and empty it out at the tunnel opening.

Train Tunnel
(South)

Service
Tunnel

Train Tunnel
(North)

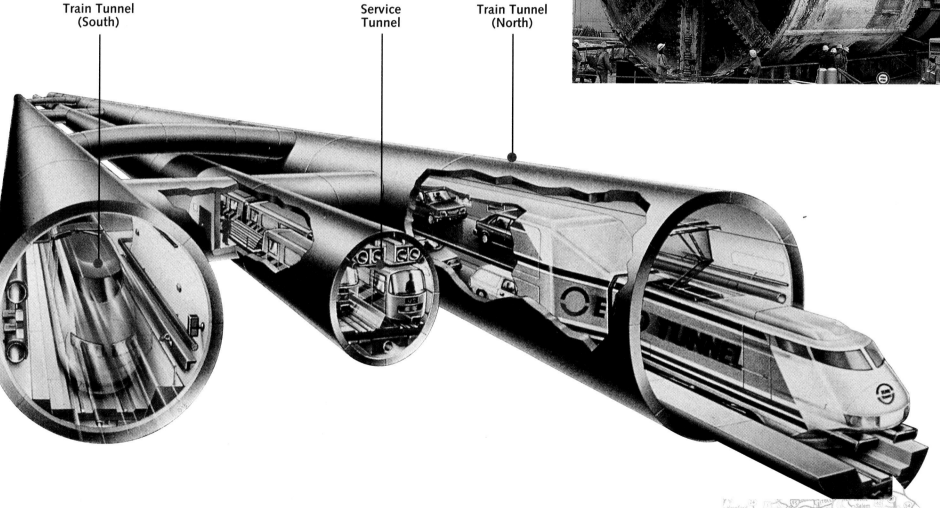

For more about
Land Transportation
GO TO PAGE 86

Water Travel ▶ Basics

Rowing

In order for watercraft to move forward, the water around them must be pushed back. In a rowboat or raft this is done with poles, oars, or paddles.

Sails

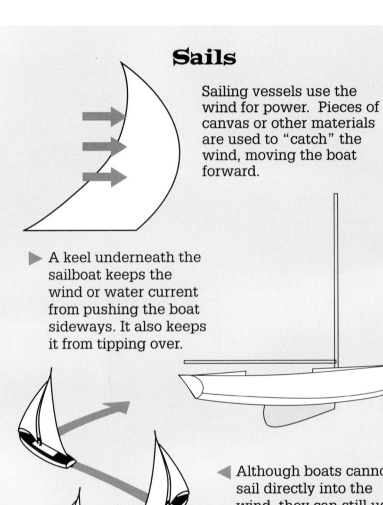

Sailing vessels use the wind for power. Pieces of canvas or other materials are used to "catch" the wind, moving the boat forward.

▶ A keel underneath the sailboat keeps the wind or water current from pushing the boat sideways. It also keeps it from tipping over.

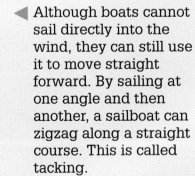

◀ Although boats cannot sail directly into the wind, they can still use it to move straight forward. By sailing at one angle and then another, a sailboat can zigzag along a straight course. This is called tacking.

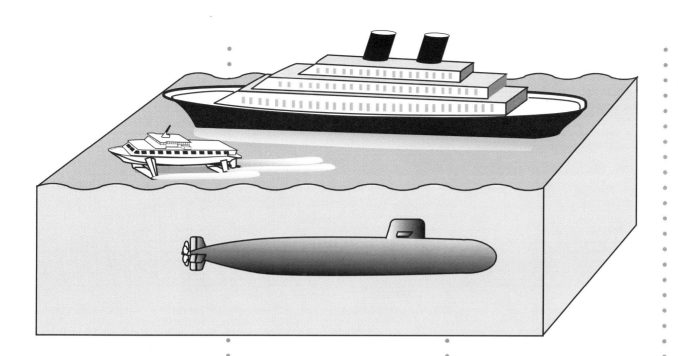

◀ Depths

Some watercraft like hydrofoils skim along the top of the water. Submarines travel underneath the water. Most boats ride along with part of their hulls in the water and part out.

▶ Propellers

Most powered craft (except hovercraft) have propeller engines that work under the water. These propellers drive the water back from the boat. As the water is pushed backward, the craft moves forward. Sometimes a kind of propeller is used inside a tube or tunnel. This is called an impeller. The impeller creates a jet of water that causes the boat to move forward. Impellers are used in jet skis, wave runners, and other craft.

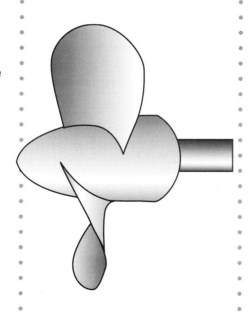

▶ Braking

Boats don't have brakes the way that land vehicles do. In order to come to a stop, a sailboat lowers its sails and turns into the wind. Powered boats stop by putting their engines briefly in reverse, or turning them off. The drag of the water along the hull will slow or stop a vessel fairly quickly.

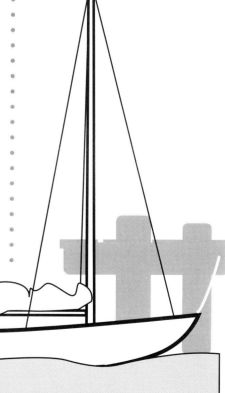

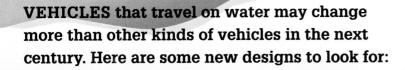
Water Travel ▶ In the Future

VEHICLES that travel on water may change more than other kinds of vehicles in the next century. Here are some new designs to look for:

Large **Cargo Vessels** **or Container Ships** will be run by computer and have only a small crew on board.

Sturdy, fuel-saving **Hovercraft** will replace boats for ferry service. They will also be used for pleasure and work boats.

The number of **Hydrofoils** will increase. Watercraft that are similar to hydrofoils, called **Jetfoils**, will also appear more.

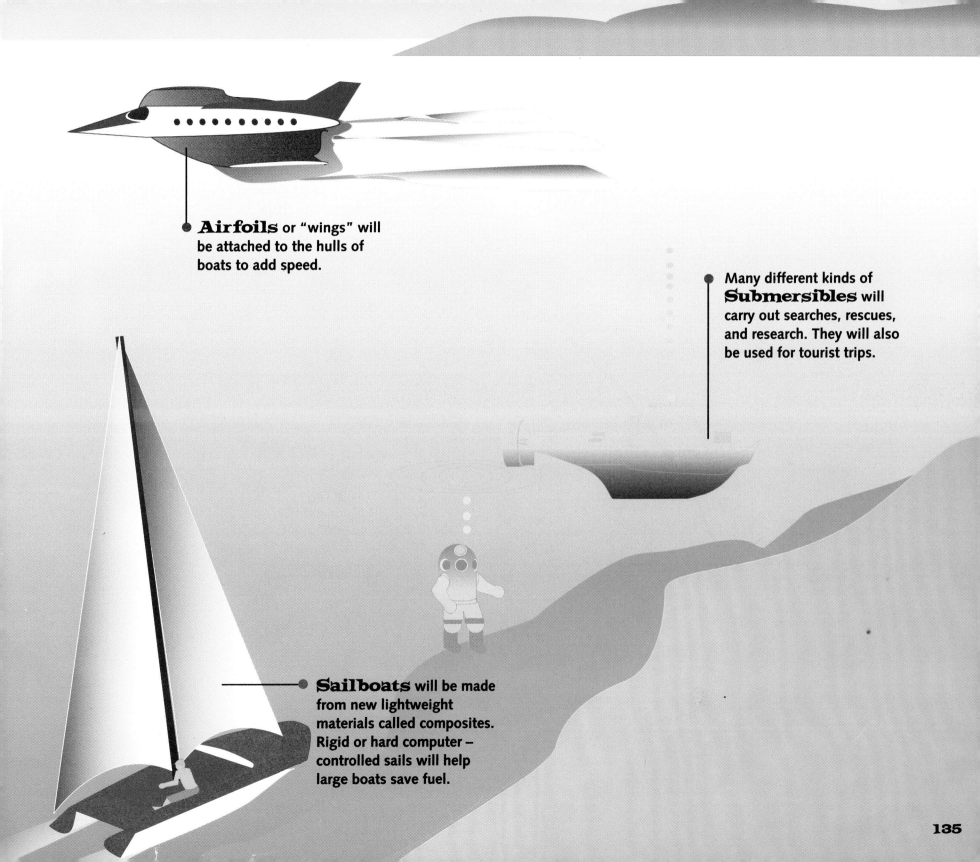

Airfoils or "wings" will be attached to the hulls of boats to add speed.

Many different kinds of **Submersibles** will carry out searches, rescues, and research. They will also be used for tourist trips.

Sailboats will be made from new lightweight materials called composites. Rigid or hard computer – controlled sails will help large boats save fuel.

Wheelchairs

MOST people start their travels in some sort of "wheeled chair." It may be a baby carriage, a stroller, or a walker. As we grow, our legs usually take over the job of moving us around. But for many people, walking can be a problem. They may have a disability or may be too weak to use their legs for transportation. For these people, wheelchairs or scooters are the answer.

A basic wheelchair has a seat with large drive wheels. A hand rim allows the person in the chair to move the drive wheels by himself or herself. Wheelchairs may have a variety of other attachments depending on the needs of the person using them. Most have leg rests, armrests, and a support for the feet.

Wheelchairs without electric power can be pushed along by the person in the chair or a helper. Powered chairs run on large batteries. Scooters have a light motor. Both powered chairs and scooters can be directed with a joystick, a lever for steering.

New wheelchairs can be specially fitted to make the rider comfortable. And modern "ultralight" chairs are extra efficient. They use the same lightweight materials that go into aircraft.

Wheelchair Competition
Wheelchair races can be fierce. Competitors use tough stainless steel chairs for speed and endurance.

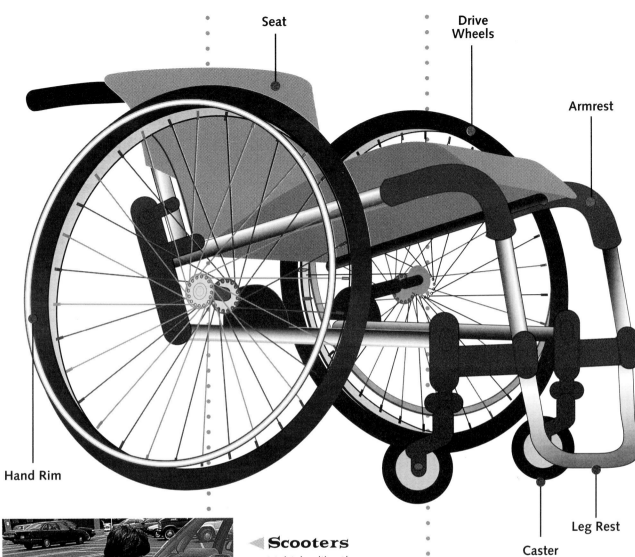

Seat

Drive
Wheels

Armrest

Hand Rim

Leg Rest

Caster
Wheels

▲ Wheelchair Design

A hang glider leaves his wheel-chair behind to take to the skies. Modern ultralight wheelchairs owe a lot of their technology to aircraft design.

◄ Scooters

Vehicles like these provide excellent mobility for people with disabilities. They are powered by electricity and can travel about 5 miles per hour.

For more about
Land Transportation
GO TO PAGE 86

Glossary

acetate Fabric or yarn made by treating plant fibers with a type of acid.

aerodynamic Designed to move through the air easily and quickly.

aileron A flap at the rear edge of an aircraft wing that the pilot uses to control the aircraft's movement.

air bag A plastic bag built into a car in front of where the riders sit. During an accident, the bag fills with air to protect the riders from injury.

air cushion vehicle (ACV) A vehicle, such as a hovercraft, that is supported above the ground by a layer of air.

airfoil A surface, such as an airplane wing, that helps a vehicle rise above the ground by controlling the direction of the flow of air.

air pollution Chemicals and particles in the air that can hurt humans, animals, and plants.

alcohol A liquid, sometimes used as fuel, that has no color or smell and catches fire easily.

arch A curved structure designed to support a bridge.

atmosphere The gases that surround a planet. Earth's atmosphere is mostly made up of nitrogen and oxygen.

axle The bar under a vehicle to which its wheels are attached.

ballast A heavy material used in water vehicles and air balloons to keep them balanced or steady, or in some cases to help them move up and down.

banking Tilting an aircraft with one wing higher than the other in order to turn.

bathyscaphe A small diving craft used for deep-sea research.

battery A container that stores chemicals which produce electricity.

beacon A light used to warn or guide a vehicle such as a plane or boat.

bit The metal piece of a bridle that is put into a horse's mouth.

bridle The headgear, including the bit and reins, that a rider uses to guide a horse.

buoy A floating marker that is used to warn or guide boats and ships.

cable A very strong rope, usually made of many wires twisted together.

cantilever A beam or support that is fastened to a wall or pier at only one end.

caravel A type of small, fast sailing ship, usually with three masts, developed by Spain and Portugal in the fifteenth century (1400s).

carbon A chemical element found in diamonds and coal and in all plants and animals.

cargo Goods carried by a ship, airplane, truck, or other vehicle.

caster wheel A small, swiveled roller used to move heavy objects more easily.

catapult A device for launching a plane from the deck of an aircraft carrier.

catenary A cable hanging between two fixed points.

cleat A shoe with pointed pieces of rubber or metal underneath that grip the ground.

cockpit The section in an airplane for the pilot and copilot.

combustion The process of burning and giving off heat energy, especially in an engine.

composite Something that is made of a mixture of plastic and other materials, like glass or metal.

compressor A machine that presses gases into a smaller space.

crankshaft The main driving rod of an engine.

cushion Something that protects against force or shock.

density How closely packed together something is.

derailleur The device on a bicycle that shifts gears by moving a chain from one gearwheel to another.

design A plan or sketch that serves as a guide or pattern. Also, to make such a plan or sketch.

diagram A drawing or outline that shows the parts of something or how something is put together.

diesel engine An engine that burns fuel oil using heat produced by compressing air.

diesel fuel A thick fuel, used in diesel engines, which is heavier than gasoline.

dock A platform built out over the water or along the shore where boats can be tied up.

drag The force that slows an object down as it moves through the air or water.

dredge A machine used to deepen a harbor or waterway by scooping up mud or sand from the bottom.

drive wheel A wheel whose movement causes another machine part to move. In an escalator, a drive wheel moves a continuous chain that is attached to a set of moving stairs.

dumbwaiter A small elevator used to carry food, dishes, or other items from one floor of a building to another.

dynamite A substance that explodes with great force and is used to blast rock.

economical Making the best possible use of a resource (fuel, for example).

efficient Something, such as a vehicle, which does its work with the least amount of waste.

electricity A form of power that occurs in nature but can also be produced by machines. Electricity can be used to run motors and produce light and heat.

elevated train A train that runs on tracks built on supports that rise above the ground.

elevator A movable part on the tail of an airplane that is used to steer the plane up or down. Also, a platform or car that moves people or things from one level to another.

energy The power from electricity and other sources which makes machines work.

engine A machine that burns fuel to release energy. Also, the front part of a train that pulls all the cars behind it.

engineer A person who is trained to build things such as bridges, roads, or airplanes. Also, a person who drives a train.

envelope The part of airships and air balloons that holds hot air or helium.

environment The natural world of land, water, and air.

exhaust The escape of used steam or gas from an engine.

expand To increase in size. Many substances expand when they are heated.

ferry A boat or ship used to carry people, cars, and goods across a stretch of water.

fiber A thin strand or thread of a material.

fiberglass Fine strands of glass spun into yarn or pressed into plastic.

fin A fixed, vertical blade attached to an aircraft to help keep it steady.

flexible Able to bend without breaking.

friction The force that slows objects down when they rub against each other.

fuselage The main body of an airplane.

gasohol A fuel that blends gasoline (usually 90 percent) and alcohol (usually 10 percent).

gauge The distance between rails on a railroad track.

gravity The force that pulls objects toward the ground.

hang glider A small glider that looks like a kite, and is steered by the pilot as he or she hangs from the aircraft's framework.

harness An arrangement of straps used to attach an animal to a wagon or to keep people safe. Rock climbers and hang gliders use harnesses.

helium A light, colorless, odorless gas used to inflate balloons and airships.

hold An area in a ship or airplane where cargo is stored.

hull The frame or body of a ship.

hydraulic Machines that are operated by liquid being forced through pipes under pressure.

hydrogen A colorless, odorless gas that catches fire easily.

hydroplane A racing powerboat that skims the surface of the water.

impeller A propeller that is set inside a tube or tunnel and is used to make vehicles move through water or air.

internal combustion engine An engine that burns its fuel internally, or inside itself. Jet engines, gasoline engines, and diesel engines are all internal combustion engines.

keel The main wooden or steel piece that runs all along the bottom of a boat and holds it together.

kerosene A thin petroleum fuel used in some engines.

laboratory A room or place used for scientific work.

lift The upward force produced by aircraft wings, helicopter rotors, and the foils of a hydrofoil.

lock Part of a canal with gates at each end where ships are raised or lowered to different water levels.

locomotive A vehicle that runs on its own power and is used to move railroad cars.

Mach number A number that tells the speed of a vehicle in relation to the speed of sound.

mast A wood or metal pole that stands on the deck of a boat and supports its sails.

maximum The greatest number possible.

mock-up A full-sized model.

monorail A train that runs on a single rail.

motor A machine that turns energy into motion.

nuclear fuel An element whose atoms are split to produce nuclear power. Uranium and plutonium are two nuclear fuels.

orbit The natural path followed by a spacecraft or other object circling a planet or the sun.

oxygen A colorless, odorless gas found in the air that humans and animals need to live.

pack ice A single mass of floating ice formed when lots of smaller pieces were pressed and frozen together.

pantograph The framework on the roof of an electric vehicle that connects with an overhead electric wire.

parachute A large piece of cloth that opens to an umbrella shape and is used to drop people, vehicles, or other objects safely from the sky to Earth.

piston A piece of metal fitted inside a cylinder that can move up and down.

platform A raised, flat surface.

pollution Damage to the environment caused by human activities.

pontoon A floating object used to hold up a bridge, a raft, or an airplane.

port A place where boats or ships are secured and protected from storms. A harbor.

pressure The force produced when one thing presses on another.

propane A colorless gas that burns easily and is often used as a fuel.

propeller A device with spinning blades that moves a vehicle through air or water.

pulley A wheel with a grooved rim that pulls a rope, cable, or chain to make lifting loads easier.

radar A system that uses radio waves to locate solid objects.

reaction An action in response to something.

recumbent Leaning back or lying down.

resistance A force that slows down something in motion.

resource Any material that is useful or valuable to a person or place.

rigging The ropes and other lines used on a boat to work the sails.

rotor A set of revolving blades that lifts an aircraft (especially a helicopter) and keeps it in flight.

rudder A vertical flap at the back of a boat or an aircraft that is used to steer the vehicle to the left or right.

rural Having to do with farming or country life.

satellite A spacecraft or a body, such as Earth's moon, that follows a path around another body in space.

sledge A sled.

solar energy Energy collected from sunlight and changed into electricity.

sonar An instrument that uses sound waves and their echoes to locate objects in water.

sonic boom A loud noise that results when an aircraft travels at or above the speed of sound.

sound barrier A sudden increase in the force of air against an object as it approaches the speed of sound.

spacecraft A vehicle designed to travel in space.

span The distance between the end supports of a bridge.

sprocket A wheel with a toothed edge, usually turned by a moving chain.

stabilizer A device used to keep airplanes and ships steady in rough air or water.

statistics Numerical information.

steam The form water takes when it is heated and turns into a gas. Steam is used to power some vehicles.

steering column The long cylinder that connects a vehicle's steering wheel to the parts that control its wheels.

structure Anything that is built, such as a tower, bridge, or pier.

subway A railroad, usually electric, that runs under the ground.

superhighway A highway with several lanes that is designed for high-speed traffic.

supersonic Traveling faster than the speed of sound.

synthetic Not made by nature, artificial.

technology Using scientific discoveries to do practical things.

temperature The measure of how hot or cold something is.

tether To tie up something (such as an animal) so that it can't move far.

thermal A rising current of warm air.

thrust The force that moves a jet or a rocket forward.

tiller A handle for turning the rudder of a boat.

traction The force of friction that holds a moving vehicle to the ground and keeps it from slipping.

traditional Following an idea or custom passed down from one generation to another.

traffic Cars, airplanes, ships, or people moving along a route.

tread The ridges on the surface of a tire that keep it from slipping.

truss A structure of beams and rods, usually made up of triangular shapes, that holds up a bridge or other platform.

turbine Any engine that is driven by water, steam, or gas passing through the blades of a wheel and making it turn.

urban Having to do with cities or city life.

vehicle Anything used to move people or things from one place to another.

vessel A ship or large boat.

waterway A river, canal, or other body of water that is used as a route for ships and boats.

waterwheel A wheel turned by flowing or falling water.

wharf A platform built along the shore or over the water where boats can unload or be tied up. A dock.

Index